PROMINENT CHRISTIAN WOMEN *The* SHARE...

GREATEST LESSON

I'VE EVER LEARNED

VONETTE ZACHARY BRIGHT
Editor

Salmon Creek United
Methodist Church

NewLife
PUBLICATIONS

The Greatest Lesson I've Ever Learned

Published by
New*Life* Publications
A ministry of Campus Crusade for Christ
P.O. Box 620877
Orlando, FL 32862-0877

Design and production by Genesis Group

Printed in the United States of America

Library of Congress Cataloging-in-Publication Data

"The greatest lesson I've ever learned" : / inspirational stories from prominent Christian women / Vonette Zachary Bright, editor.
    p. cm.
    ISBN 1-56399-085-7
    1. Christian biography—United States. 2. Women—United States—Biography.
3. Women—Religious life. 4. Christian life—Anecdotes.
I. Bright, Vonette Z.
BRI713.G74   1990
209'.2'2—dc 20
[B]   90-35743
                                            CIP

Scripture quotations are from:

The *New International Version,* © 1973, 1978, 1984 by the International Bible
    Society. Published by Zondervan Bible Publishers, Grand Rapids, Michigan

The Living Bible, © 1971 by Tyndale House Publishers, Wheaton, Illinois

The New American Standard Bible, © 1960, 1962, 1963, 1968, 1971, 1972, 1973,
    1975, 1977 by the Lockman Foundation, La Habra, California

The *New King James Version,* © 1982 by Thomas Nelson, Inc., Nashville,
    Tennessee

The *King James Version*

For more information, write:

Australia Campus Crusade for Christ—P.O. Box 40, Flemington Markets,
    NSW 2129, Australia
Campus Crusade for Christ of Canada—Box 529, Sumas, WA 98295

Agape—Fairgate House, King's Road, Tyseley, Birmingham, B11 2AA, United Kingdom

Campus Crusade for Christ—P.O. Box 8786, Auckland, 1035, New Zealand

Campus Crusade for Christ—9 Lock Road #03-03, Paccan Centre, Singapore 108937

Great Commission Movement of Nigeria—P.O. Box 500, Fudaya Village, Bauchi Ring Road, Jos, Plateau State, Nigeria, West Africa

Campus Crusade for Christ International—100 Lake Hart Drive, Orlando, FL 32832, USA

To my husband, Bill, who is a constant
encouragement, and
to all of these women who have been
open and honest in sharing their greatest
lessons to make this book possible

Contents

To the Reader

Elise and Patrick were married in a beautiful traditional Christian ceremony, which ended with the lighting of a single candle. They took candles, which their mothers had previously lit to represent each of their families, and joined their flames to light the wick of the single candle that signified the beginning of their lives together. Each then blew out the flame of his own candle.

During the wedding reception, the father of the bride asked the guests to come to the microphone and share with the young couple any admonition, memories, funny stories, or comments they desired. He also asked that they would say a prayer of blessing for the bride and groom after their remarks.

I have attended a thousand or more weddings, but this was a new and very interesting approach to launching a young couple in the formation of a new home.

As the bride and groom listened to each statement—some humorous, some serious, but all very meaningful—and as person after person prayed God's blessing upon them, I began to consider how different, and even bizarre, this experience could seem to many people who know little or nothing about the biblical approach to marriage.

It also has become strange to some people to approach solutions to problems from a biblical point of view. "The Bible says…" is not as known or relevant in our "enlightened" age as it once was. The standards of the Bible are at odds with the standards of the world.

I became all the more aware of this recently when I was reading the Beatitudes that Jesus gave in His Sermon on the Mount, recorded in Matthew 5: "'Humble men are very fortunate!' he told them, 'for the Kingdom of Heaven is given to them. Those who mourn are fortunate! for they shall be comforted. The meek and lowly are fortunate! for the whole wide world belongs to them. Happy are those who long to be just and good, for they shall be completely satisfied. Happy are the kind and merciful, for they shall be shown mercy. Happy are those whose hearts are pure, for they shall see God. Happy are those who strive for peace— they shall be called the sons of God. Happy are those who are persecuted because they are good, for the Kingdom of Heaven is theirs'" (Matthew 5:3–10).

The footnote in the *Life Application Bible* says this:

> Jesus began His sermon with words that seemed to contradict each other. But God's way of living usually contradicts the world's. If you want to live for God, you must be ready to say and do what seems strange to the world. You must be willing to give when others take, to love when others hate, to help when others abuse. In doing this you will one day receive everything, while the others will end up with nothing.

The book you now hold contains living examples of women who have chosen to live within the boundaries of God's textbook to mankind, the Bible.

Why listen to people like this? These women of experience have found answers to human needs, to which so often there seems to be no answer. And don't we *all* have needs! A need for love, a need for security, a need for forgiveness, a need for self-esteem, a need for wisdom!

In sharing with you how they coped with real-life situations, these women give you examples of how to live from their knowledge of the Bible and their walk with God. I trust they will bless your life as they have mine.

Vonette Zachary Bright,
Editor

Ney Bailey

IS MY GOD BIGGER THAN MY HURT?

A former adoption agency case worker in New Orleans, Ney Bailey has been a staff member with Campus Crusade for Christ for nearly forty years. Presently, she is an international traveling representative with this ministry.

After serving on campus at the University of Arizona, she founded and directed Campus Crusade's personnel department for six years. She has spoken extensively on university campuses, at weekend conferences and retreats, and to civic groups. Ney has also addressed congressional wives, ambassadors, and diplomats.

She participated in the founding of Campus Crusade's Family Ministry and Keystone Kaper Singles' Conference, initiated Campus Crusade's Alumni Ministry, and has served on the faculty of the Institute of Biblical Studies. She also serves on the board of directors of Insight for Living, Dr. Charles R. Swindoll's ministry.

She is listed in The World Who's Who of Women *and is the author of the best-selling book* Faith Is Not a Feeling.

A good listener, wise counselor, and excellent speaker, Ney readily identifies with her audience whether it be one person or thousands.

I was barely three feet tall and standing on the edge of the municipal swimming pool.

"Jump, Ney Ann!" coaxed my father, his arms out-stretched. "I'll catch you!"

The water was over my head where he was standing in the pool and I was petrified about jumping in.

Trembling, I called out, "No, I can't do it."

"Yes, you can," he shouted. "Jump, and I'll catch you!"

Finally, I jumped. My head went under the water and I came up sputtering and thrashing. My father wasn't there. He had moved back in the water, hoping I would swim to him. I began to cry.

"Daddy, you moved! You said you wouldn't!"

I heard him laughing.

"Ney Ann, you've gotten upset over nothing. You know I wouldn't let anything happen to you. I was just trying to teach you to swim."

That experience had a devastating effect on my tender, young mind. I had trusted Daddy with everything that my little heart could muster—he had said he would catch me, but he didn't. He had let me down.

This experience represents how I began to feel about my

father as I grew older. I began to realize that some of the deepest hurts we'll ever know come from those we care most about, hurts that often result in bruised relationships within our families. And those relationships are often the hardest to heal. With many other experiences to fuel my feelings and attitudes, my bitterness toward my father became deeply rooted—and was fully grown—by the time I entered college.

In later years, my hostility turned to a subtle rebellion. I thought, *You go your way and I'll go mine. You don't bother me and I won't bother you.* If Dad yelled at me, I wished I could yell back. If he ignored me, I ignored him. If he hurt my feelings, I'd try to hurt his. I wanted to give him what I thought he deserved.

When I was fifteen, I invited Jesus Christ to become my Savior, but it wasn't until I had graduated from college and was working in New Orleans that I truly gave my life to Christ. At twenty-five, I joined the staff of Campus Crusade for Christ.

As I became an adult, my relationship with my dad was not characterized by open hostility, but it did lack warmth and understanding. We politely went our separate ways. I felt no guilt or loss. I assume he didn't either.

Later, my discovery of the meaning of faith was a catalyst that led to the improvement in my relationship with my dad.

One summer I was taking a class on the Book of Romans. One of my assignments was to go through Romans and find everything Paul said about faith.

As I moved through the chapters, the word "faith" appeared almost too many times to count. As I pondered the word, I found myself asking, "What is it? Faith is probably the most important thing in my life, but how do I define it?"

I thought, *Lord, how would You define it?*

Immediately a story came to mind in which Jesus had said to someone, "Not even in Israel have I found such great faith." I became quite curious. What was it that Jesus Himself called "great faith"?

I quickly looked up the passage in Luke 7, and learned that He equated great faith with someone who was simply willing to take Him at His word.

I wondered if such a "definition" would be confirmed elsewhere in Scripture. Since Hebrews 11 is often referred to as "faith's hall of fame," I turned there.

For example, God told Noah to build an ark.

Noah took God at His word and built the ark. Therefore, Hebrews 11:7 begins, "By faith Noah..." Throughout the chapter it appeared that regardless of the circumstances, despite arguments of logic and reason—even regardless of how he felt—each person believed God, took Him at His word, and chose to be obedient.

By now, my homework had become far more exciting than I could have imagined.

On the basis of all I observed in these passages, I had arrived at a simple, workable definition of faith! I wasn't sure if I would ever finish the assignment on all that the Book of Romans said about faith, but in my own heart I knew I had learned something that would prove to be very significant in my walk with God.

But I had one more question: If faith is a matter of taking God at His word, what does God say *about* His Word? I found the answer in Scripture itself:

"The word of the Lord abides forever" (1 Peter 1:25).

"The grass withers, the flower fades, but the word of our God stands forever" (Isaiah 40:8).

"Heaven and earth will pass away, but My words shall not pass away" (Matthew 24:35).

Everything in life may change, I observed, but God's Word remains constant! That means:

- God's Word is truer than anything I feel.
- God's Word is truer than anything I experience.
- God's Word is truer than any circumstance I will ever face.
- God's Word is truer than anything in the world.

I began to see clearly that faith is not a feeling, it is a choice we have—to take God at His word. As a result, I made a lifetime commitment to bank my life on God's Word.

I was beginning to catch a glimpse of how this could affect me, and for the first time in my life, I began to think about the impact of my faith on my relationship with my father.

I had always heard that I was supposed to love other people with a 1 Corinthians 13 kind of love. Someone suggested that I test my love for others by inserting my name wherever the chapter mentions "love." For example: "Ney is patient, Ney is kind, Ney is not provoked…" I failed the test! Then I remembered 1 John 4:16 says that God is love. And since 1 Corinthians 13 explains what love is, I decided to put God's name beside the word "love" and relate it to myself:

- God's love toward me is patient,
- God's love toward me is kind,
- God's love toward me is not provoked,

17

- God's love toward me does not take into account a wrong suffered,
- God's love toward me would bear all things,
- believe all things,
- hope all things,
- endure all things.
- God's love toward me would never fail.

It was overwhelming to think that He loved me in that way. And I was struck with amazement to realize that He loved my father in the very same way.

I thought, *If God loves my father just the way he is, who am I not to love him also?* My love had been conditional, based on his performance. I had been waiting for him to change. Then, if he changed, I would begin to love him.

My love had said, "Daddy, I'll love you if you do this and if you do that." Yet God's love simply said, "I love you, *period.*" No "if's" about it.

I was driving up the mountain road to my home with tears streaming down my face as the reality of this truth began touching my heart. For the first time in my life, I decided to take God at His word and love and accept my father just as he was.

I was grateful for this new understanding as I pulled the car into my driveway. It seemed as if the Lord had done something new in my life. But I knew the real test was yet to come.

Not knowing where to begin, I began to pray that God would give me an opportunity to make things right with my father. I knew it would be difficult and that I would not feel like doing it, but I needed to take the first step.

The next time I visited my folks, I had an attitude of

love and acceptance rather than one of being critical and judgmental. As I was nice to my father, he was nice to me. He must have sensed God's Spirit working in me.

Later, I remember thinking, *If my dad were to die, would I have any regrets at his funeral?* The answer was "Yes." I would regret that I had never asked him to forgive me for some of my ugly ways while I was growing up.

So, I purposed in my heart to ask his forgiveness. It was very scary to talk to him because he was a bullheaded lawyer, by his own description, and I imagined myself prostrate on the ground, crying my eyes out, unable to say a word.

On the weekend I went home, I knew enough not to talk to him during the football game, so I waited for half-time and for my mother to leave the room. When he and I were alone I said, "Daddy, I've been thinking about my growing-up years—how unloving, ungrateful, and unkind I was. Will you forgive me?"

IF GOD LOVES MY FATHER JUST THE WAY HE IS, WHO AM I NOT TO LOVE HIM ALSO?

As he turned and looked at me with a twinkle in his eye, he said, "No." Pausing, he added, "I don't remember

all those things except for the time…" And then he named one.

Knowing the importance of his response, I asked, "Will you forgive me for what you can remember?"

"Yes," he answered.

From that time on he was warmer and kinder than ever before.

Without warning, a few years later my father became

critically ill.

As I was leaving his bedside in the intensive care unit, I said, "Well, Daddy, I'd better go now and let Brenda [my sister] come in. She's out in the hall waiting. I love you, Daddy."

"I love you, too, honey, whether you're in here or whether you're out in the hall waiting to come in." Those were to be his last words to me.

A few days later as the family gathered at the funeral home, I looked out and saw the casket. I remembered that when I did not feel like it, I chose with my will to forgive my father. I was so glad as I was sitting there that I did not have any regrets. The only regret I did have was that I had not done it sooner.

I realized that when I am hurt I need to ask myself the question, "Is my God bigger than my hurt or is my hurt bigger than my God?" I am the one who gets to choose. There are many things that are inexcusable, but nothing is unforgivable. Someone has said, "To forgive is to set the prisoner free only to discover that the prisoner was you." I am not most like Christ when I am perfect, but I am most like Christ when I am forgiving.

My dad never asked me to forgive him, but God asked that of me and it made all the difference.[1]

Jill Briscoe

THE ULTRA-SUEDE LADIES

Jill Briscoe is real, practical, down-to-earth, and disarmingly honest with a well-adjusted, healthy outlook on her gifts, family, and ministry.

Born in Liverpool, England, and educated at Homerton College in Cambridge, she is an advisor to the women's ministries at the Elmbrook Church in Brookfield, Wisconsin, where her husband, Stuart, is the pastor. They minister together through their "Telling the Truth" media outreach.

Jill is executive editor of Just Between Us, *a magazine for ministry wives and women in leadership, and advises numerous non-profit organizations.*

Because of her heart for God, she is helping women wherever she travels to overcome their feelings of inadequacy. She joyfully helps them do the things they never believed they could do and be the people they never thought they could be. The following story relates how she overcame her own lack of self-confidence and how God began to develop in her a new sense of well-being.

"I had tea with the Queen," the beautiful lady informed me.

"Queen who?" I wanted to ask facetiously. But I knew "who." Queen Elizabeth, of course. *My* queen! This polished American lady who was to share the platform with me at a women's retreat was telling me all about her tea party with the Queen of England herself! After describing the event in detail, the lady added another story of yet one more "queenly" interview in another European capital, where she had been able to actually talk to "Her Majesty" about the Lord!

Settling back in the big black limousine that was speeding us toward the retreat center, I thought of how I had never even seen the Queen in person, never mind had tea with her. How absolutely marvelous! I envisioned myself in Buckingham Palace, standing in this huge room under a gigantic chandelier, holding a white Bible in my hand. I would know *just* the right thing to say to the royal relatives; I would be in complete charge of myself and the situation. Carried away with such fantasies, I could see the Royal Guards bowing their black fuzzy hats in prayer as they stood in their compact little boxes outside the palace gate.

I was brought back to earth by the beautiful lady inquiring, "And just where have *you* been lately?"

I gazed at her, completely lost for words. I wanted to say casually, "Oh, Washington, D.C., a little Bible study meeting with the congressmen's wives, and then on to the Florida Hilton, before dropping in for a quick meeting at the governor's mansion!" I wanted to say it but couldn't—though all of those invitations had been given to me, I hadn't accepted them. Looking at my beautiful ultra-suede companion, I felt the old familiar struggle all over again. *I wanted to be like her!*

Ultra-suede ladies, especially the ultra-ultra ones, frightened me out of my mind. I had already decided there was absolutely no way that God could use me to reach "the up and outers."

Just look at me, I mumbled quietly as I slumped against the upholstery in a self-conscious heap. *Here I am in my forties, suffering from a teenage bad self-image syndrome.* I wanted to shout at my Maker, "Why don't You recall all those 1935 models with defects [like me] and make us right! For a start, You could give me new hair."

My hair was the fine baby type that convinced me I faced premature baldness. Often I was tempted to get on a plane with a plastic bag over my head so the wind wouldn't mess up my painstakingly arranged hairdo. It was years before I could travel comfortably.

Sitting in the speeding limousine beside my American friend, I also pondered why the Eternal hadn't made my metabolism so that I could eat all those sweet, sticky, energy-giving cakes and hot fudge sundaes that I wanted and still stay slim and trim! I found myself starving after each speech, craving for an extra shot of energy to meet a demanding traveling schedule. When I stayed in a private home, people were just too kind in their care of me. How do you refuse your hostess's lovingly prepared caloric recipes without offending her? And anyway, who *wants* to refuse?

Glancing sideways in the semi-dark cab, I acknowledged the super-trim shape of my companion with something akin to gloom and despair. How would I ever gain the ear of the ultra, ultra-suede ladies unless I looked like a size-eight model?

"And then, Lord, there is the money problem," I sighed. "How could I ever afford to dress ultra-suede to match my audience, or on the other hand cope with the trouble arising if I did?" For one thing, the ultra, ultra-suede who seemed to put such store in appearance might not listen if I didn't match up dress-wise, but then the "sub-suede" in the audience (like me!) might consider an ultra-suede outfit a gross misuse of the Lord's money!

I remembered with a shudder the time I found myself a guest in an incredible "villa." We were to change for dinner in a "small" bedroom (about half the size of our entire house). The other ladies were pouring themselves into their exclusive outfits and throwing around the casual remarks about Dior's latest show! With my little bit of starched cotton dress hanging limply from my hand, I encountered a fabulous-looking creature who remarked kindly, "That looks like a pretty little creation, Jill." She had focused the attention of the entire roomful of women onto my apparel. I didn't need to say it, but I did anyway. "Sears," I whispered, as if I'd just been caught shoplifting! *Why did I do that?* I asked myself furiously. Why couldn't I just smile and say "thank you," because it *was* a pretty dress and quite as lovely as all the rest, just not as expensive.

I knew in my heart, of course, that my reaction was a guilty confession to these women that, because of the way I looked, I felt totally out of place among them. How could it be that I still believed those ultra, ultra-suede ladies would hear what I had to say only if I dressed in ultra-suede? Maybe the fact of the matter was that this woman's ministry just wasn't my "cup of tea," as we say in England.

If your husband is a speaker, the public expects you to follow suit. *All* sorts of doors of opportunity had opened up to me as soon as I arrived in the States, simply because of Stuart's already well-established ministry.

"But I don't *want* to speak to ladies," I had complained to the Eternal. He knew I never had liked it when lots of women were compressed together in a confined space. What a row they made for starters! But having learned not to be a Jonah and run away from my responsibility to speak to people whom I didn't particularly like, I had answered the invitations and gone anyway.

It really doesn't matter that I don't like them very much, I thought. *After all, they needn't know!*

Like Jonah, I marched into Nineveh (the situation I would like to have stayed away from) and preached my heart out —retiring like that same angry prophet to my hill of disdain once the engagement was over. But God apparently used the message and I received requests to return.

One day I went to Memphis, Tennessee. Verla met me at the airport. She was a speaker and teacher, ran a rescue mission, talked to up-and-outers and down-and-outers, and was totally relaxed with both. She gave me an uncomfortable feeling in the pit of my conscience the moment I saw her warm touch with the women. Her whole approach and ministry served to rebuke me outright, saying louder than any verbal complaint: "Jill, you are technically a good speaker, but *you do not love these women!*"

Being with her was like telling me my slip was showing, only this was the slip of disobedience, and it was hanging down several inches. I knew that love was a conscious decision, and where these women were concerned I had definitely decided against love.

The Eternal had long since shown me that love was not just a feeling too big for words. Jesus had said to His followers, "A new commandment I give unto you, that ye love one another" (John 13:34). I knew that you couldn't command a feeling, and so had come to the conclusion that if love was a command, I must be able to obey it. This took love out of the realm of emotions and into the arena of loving actions. And that would involve me in the lives of people I didn't "feel" I liked!

I HAD COME TO THE CONCLUSION THAT IF LOVE WAS A COMMAND, I MUST BE ABLE TO OBEY IT.

God could help me to love them, I decided, but *that* wasn't the issue. The problem was, would they love *me*, and most important, would they listen to what I had to tell them?

Once I was on my feet with my Bible open and a message prepared, I felt fine. It was the before and after small talk, the winning-of-the-ladies-to-myself-that-I-might-win-them-to-Him part that got to me!

What I was like *off* the platform was a question those women had every right to ask. If they knew my insecurities, if they heard my foolish attempts at making classy conversation, I knew they would dislike me.

As our limousine continued toward our destination, I groaned inwardly, thinking of the disappointment the women were in for as they found out there was "nothing to me" after all!

Stuart had encouraged me to take this particular invitation. He had reminded me of the apostle Paul counting himself in debt to the Jew and the Greek, barbarian and free. That, he explained, meant we all had a debt to pay— that of sharing the knowledge of salvation with all types of people, including the sophisticated as well as the unsophisticated. Believing it, I had simply come to pay my debt.

All too soon, the taxi arrived. The meetings came and went, and I returned home just as unsure of everything as I had been when I set out.

In the days that followed, I asked myself if it was simply my Britishness that forbade the crossing of the "class" line, or if my problem was just inverted pride. Perhaps it was false humility or a despising of the gifts that others saw in me. I didn't know what was so dreadfully wrong, so I continued to travel and speak and wonder afterward how on earth I'd had the nerve!

Then one day the Eternal decided it was time to set me free. I was in Coral Gables, Florida, among some of the *nouveau riche* young ladies who populate that classy area of Miami. Observing them as they entered the club restaurant where we were dining, each one seemed a beauty in her own lovely right.

Sitting at a table with three of the most elegant females, I felt fat, forty, and somewhat futile! Why, oh, why had I come?

I looked around at the beautiful exclusive-looking creature who had just made her entrance from an exclusive car into that exclusive place and was about to order some of their exclusive food at a definitely exclusive price! Suddenly and unexpectedly the Eternal inquired of me, "Why do you think everyone is so tense?"

"Competition," I replied with sudden comprehension.

"That's right," He answered.

It was very, very still in my heart, so I distinctly heard the Eternal's next words: "Jill, you'll *never* be competition."

That was it—I was *free!* Oh, the joy of it. I could be a big sister to them, a friendly mother to them, an ugly aunt to them. But certainly I could relax, knowing I would never threaten one of them! They were bound to listen to me for the very reason I had believed them bound not to! What an incredible release!

God had made me just right for my vocation, and that was all that mattered. He had gifted me with ordinary and acceptable good looks. Everywhere I went, someone would always come up to me and tell me I was like their daughter, cousin, or Great Aunt Susan. Now I could see how comfortable that made everybody feel.

I thanked God for dressing me well enough to hold my own, but not too well to distract or cause envy, freeing me to wear an outfit twice in a row if I desired. For the first time I was able to be glad for my fine hair, realizing that because it curled so easily I could always bully it into shape.

I began to make a mental list of my best qualities. I had a sort of pleasant voice (that made a long talk part-way enjoyable), an expressive face (useful for dramatic emphasis), and a metabolism that could be mastered by diet and discipline. To discover you are "just right" in His eyes is enough. *He* is the lover of our souls, and to despise the way He has assembled our bodies, dressed our heads, or arranged our features is to miss the point. To be able to say, "I am free, not to be the me that *I* would choose to be, but the me *He* has already chosen me to be," is freedom indeed.

Set free on the outside, I was about to be set free on the

inside as well!

It was Christmas time and as I opened the Gospel of Luke I read the words of Zacharias. He prayed for all others, like himself, whose mouths had been closed by fear and doubt, by that dreadful and strangling sense of the inadequacy, when faced with God's expectations of them. He was interceding for those of us who would come to know the liberty of a God-confident self-acceptance: "May God grant that we, being delivered out of the hand of our enemies, might *serve Him without fear*." God was about to grant me just that.

I had fought this battle for so long, without victory. I had prayed earnestly for the fear to be removed, but without avail. I had even tried to dig into my subconscious to find reasons for my anxieties. I worried in preparing a talk whether it would be interesting enough. I dreaded being asked questions that I presumably wouldn't be able to answer. I also was afraid of success. Just what might praise or appreciation do to my head and therefore to my sweet relationship with the Lord?

Letters began to come from editors inviting me to write. Immediately, I felt suffocated with fear. Why write articles *nobody* will read? Hot on the heels of that anxiety came a worse dread: People would rip them apart doctrinally or write nasty letters to the editor that *everybody* would read!

With the memory of Coral Gables fresh in my mind, I took time out to listen to God. Again the Eternal applied His Word to my heart. He visited me with the written Word as He had visited Zacharias with the Living Word, and it proved to be sweeter than honey, finer than gold, more precious than rubies. He reminded me of the way He had overcome my fear of losing friends, of sharing my faith, of being attacked on the back streets of Liverpool, of something happening to the children or to Stuart and the horror of rejection and death. He had dealt with my awful fear of flying.

Even my fearful obediences had brought me great reward. They had led to marvelous adventures that I wouldn't have missed for anything. But now I knew that the promise to serve Him *without fear* was for me and had everything to do with the ultra-suede ladies.

As I knelt, the Father dressed my spirit with an incredibly tender anticipation of heavenly delight. I told the Lord Jesus how much I loved Him for it all—He who must have been tempted to be afraid many, many times; He who had refused to doubt His Father's faithfulness to Him; He who could have decided not to be a suffering servant for fear that what He went through wouldn't make a difference. But He came anyway and didn't shudder at the rejection of the world or the agony of the cross. He feared His Father first! *The fear of God, rather than the fear of man, was the key*—fear in the sense of reverent trust, coupled with hatred of sin.

Shuffling through my invitations with a quickening excitement, I chose three of the most challenging I had ever been given and wrote an eager acceptance. Surprised by a feeling of peace and an incredible new hope, I breathed, *West Point, Princeton, Washington…ultra, ultra-suede ladies, here we come!* And as I went, it was with the prayer of Psalm 19 uppermost in my thinking.

> May the words of my mouth and the meditation of my heart be acceptable *in thy sight*, oh Lord, my Rock and my Redeemer! (Psalm 19:14)

As I stood on platforms here and there and felt wooden planks or shiny bricks underneath my feet, I somehow knew I would begin to feel another substance undergirding my obedience: "my Rock." That new confidence in my Redeemer's promises would begin to work in me a new sense of well-being with myself.

My ministry took on a new swing—an exuberance, a depth of satisfaction and sureness I'd never known before. As I left a huge convention to catch a plane to the next assignment, I smiled at the jumble of cars and at my frantic hostess running around like a scalded cat—she couldn't remember where she'd parked. I was reminded of my husband's quip, "Women don't park cars, they abandon them!"

The next time some dear little blue-haired ladies in tennis shoes came and whispered in my ear, "We couldn't hear you," and I asked, "Where were you sitting?" and they answered me, "On the back row and we're all deaf you know," I found a sweet warmth and loving concern instead of the old irritation as I patiently suggested they sit on the front row next time!

It was all different. Women were everywhere. In my head, in my heart, in my plans, in my schedules and spare moments, in my tears and in my laughter—they were part of me and I was part of them. And I was *glad, glad, glad*— we were women together!¹

Barbara Bush

EVERYONE HAS
SOMETHING TO GIVE

Barbara Pierce Bush, wife of former President George Bush and the thirty-eighth First Lady, has lived a life that reflects her husband's varied career in business and public service.

The Bushes have lived in seventeen cities and twenty-nine homes since their marriage in 1945. The demands of his service as a member of Congress, U.S. Representative to the United Nations, Chairman of the Republican National Committee, Chief of the United States Liaison Office in the People's Republic of China, Director of the CIA, and Vice President and President of the United States, have truly made them public servants.

Mrs. Bush has chosen the promotion of literacy as her special area of focus. She is honorary chairperson of the Barbara Bush Foundation for Family Literacy, an organization whose mission is to establish literacy as a value in every family in America, to support the development of family literacy programs, and to break the intergenerational cycle of illiteracy.

Mrs. Bush also serves as the honorary chairperson of a number of other organizations, councils, foundations, and groups relating to education, literacy, learning disabilities, child abuse, hunger, health, and adoption.

She has received the honorary degree of Doctor of Humane Letters from several institutions, including Smith College in Northampton, Massachusetts; Bennett College in Greensboro, North Carolina; and Morehouse School of Medicine in Atlanta, Georgia.

The mother of five children and grandmother of twelve, Mrs. Bush is an exercise enthusiast and enjoys reading, gardening, and being with her family.

To celebrate the National Day of Prayer their first year in office, President and Mrs. Bush honored the National Prayer Committee at a breakfast in the White House State Dining Room. They were honorary co-chairmen for 1990.

I believe history will regard her as one of our nation's all-time great First Ladies. (America loves you, Barbara.)

Her contribution to this book reflects her heart for people and captures her refreshing philosophy of life.

During his presidency, George Bush, one of the smartest people I know, challenged the people of our great country to open their hearts to one another.

That is the way George has lived his life, and he made it a theme of his presidency when he said in a speech, "From now on, any definition of a successful life must include service to others."

It's no wonder, then, that being married to George Bush has been instrumental in teaching me what I consider my most important lesson: Caring for and sharing with others is life's biggest reward.

It is a lesson I never quit learning—sometimes through the large, significant incidents in my life; more often, through small, daily reminders such as an offhand remark or a handshake. I would like to share a few such incidents with you.

In 1953, George and I were living in Midland, Texas. We thought we were on top of the world. We were young, full of energy and ambition, with our whole lives stretching before us. George was working long hours establishing himself in the oil business. I was busy having babies and raising them. Everything seemed so right.

Then our world broke apart. One bright spring day, a doctor told us that our precious three-year-old daughter, Robin, had leukemia and would not live. Despite a brave battle and the care of many doctors, she died seven months later.

The time of her illness and death was one of the most difficult periods of my life. The death of a child is so painful, both emotionally and spiritually, that I truly wondered if my own heart and spirit would ever heal.

But our strong faith in God and our wonderful family and friends pulled us through. Everywhere we looked there were helping hands: those of good friends and family, and those of strangers—the doctors and nurses and hospital volunteers who saw our pain and reached out to us.

Through them, I soon learned that I could help myself best by helping others.

George and I came from families dedicated to volunteerism and public service, but it wasn't until Robin died that I truly threw myself into volunteer work. That precious little girl left our family a great legacy: I know George and I care more for every living person because of her. We learned firsthand the importance of reaching out to help because others had reached out to us during that crucial time.

Since then, my strong belief in volunteerism and the spirit of caring has been reinforced almost daily by the wonderful people I have met. I am talking about the "silent" heroes, the thousands of people who work hard behind the scenes to make life better for others. You will never see their names in the headlines or their faces on the evening news.

I SOON LEARNED THAT I COULD HELP MYSELF BEST BY HELPING OTHERS.

Instead, they are the people who live right next door to us, kneel next to us in church, or have children who go to school with our children and grandchildren.

They are the people who provide shelter for the homeless or take in babies afflicted with the AIDS virus. They are volunteers in hospitals and nursing homes; the tutors for children who have trouble learning and for adults who never learned to read or write.

They are the neighborhood women who get together and cook a meal for a new mother, the talented fundraiser who can find the necessary pennies for all the right causes, the class of fourth-graders who once a week make cheese sandwiches at the homeless shelter downtown.

When people ask me how they can help, what they can

possibly do to make a difference (so many people worry that they don't have the time, talent, or resources), I tell them about all of these "silent" heroes.

One of my favorites is a man I don't even know.

Not long ago, while visiting a school in Boston, I saw a blind man teaching two young boys how to read. I will never forget him—and I hope you don't either. For that very brief encounter helped remind me in a very special way of life's most important lesson: Caring and sharing is everything—and everyone has something to give.

Evelyn Christenson

"BEFORE YOU KNOW THE OUTCOME, HERE IS MY PEACE"

Evelyn Christenson is the wife of a pastor turned college administrator. She reared three children while being involved in church and denominational activities in support of her husband's ministry.

As a Bible teacher who observed firsthand what can happen when women pray, she saw the need for a united prayer movement.

I first met Evelyn when she and her husband came to Arrowhead Springs for a conference. It was early 1972, just as I was launching a movement to encourage united prayer in our nation. I shared with her how I was sure prayer could bring our nation back to a greater moral and spiritual foundation. Our hearts were immediately united, and she invited me to be one of the speakers for Bethel College Founder's Week.

Now Evelyn is the founder and chairman of the board of United Prayer Ministries in St. Paul, Minnesota. Under her direction, the ministry operates a prayer chain in the Twin City area, furnishes Christian material to missionaries around the world and to prisoners in the United States, and sponsors broadcasts into China, India, and Spanish-speaking lands.

Evelyn is the author of several books, including What Happens When Women Pray, *which has sold more than two million copies and was on the best-seller list for four consecutive years. She is one of the original members of the National Prayer Committee and co-chair of AD2000 North American Women's Track. Although in great demand as a speaker around the world, she still gives priority to her now-retired husband and loves being a grandmother.*

Her story is one of God's abiding peace in the face of cancer and how His purpose for our lives is unchangeable even when life's circumstances become difficult.

For many generations no word has struck terror in human hearts more than the word *cancer*. Somehow, pronouncing it evokes—rightly or wrongly—visions of suffering, chemotherapy, and death. Through the years, hearing it diagnosed has gripped hearts of patients and loved ones alike with icy fingers.

I struggled with that word myself. In a routine checkup, my husband's doctor found "a little lump." Later on the biopsy report was that word: *cancer*.

We had to wait several more days—until the following Monday—for his bone marrow, CT scan, and blood tests to see if the cancer had spread to other parts of his body, knowing full well what it meant if it had.

On Friday Chris and I drove to Illinois for a prayer seminar with that word hanging over us like a thick, menacing cloud. *Cancer.*

While Chris took his turn to nap and I drove, I talked to God about the word *promises* in Hebrews 6:12, which He had impressed upon me the month before:

That you may not be sluggish, but imitators of those who through faith and patience inherit the promises.

Why did the Lord place this word so heavily on my heart? What did He mean? Was He about to promise me something? Was He speaking to me about my ministry or my personal life? I didn't have the faintest idea.

I prayed fervently, pleading with God to give me more insight. Then clearly and firmly the answer came to my mind: "Romans 8:28." It was as though He were saying, "I, God, am working all things together for your good because you love Me and are called according to My purpose."

Disappointed and almost frustrated with God, I cried, "Oh God, not *that* old one again."

When I was just twenty-three years old, I lost my first three pregnancies. At that time, God had spoken words of comfort and assurance to me through Romans 8:28.

Having taken this verse then as my philosophy of life, I had lived it and God had proven faithful to it for forty-two years. But now, in the face of my husband's cancer, I wanted —and thought I needed—something new and powerful.

But as I drove, God began to impress on my heart why He had again chosen this particular promise. *Up to this time,* He said into my heart, *you have been experiencing, teaching, and writing about how I work out all things for your good because you love Me. But I want to expand your understanding of this verse. You have thought that you will see Me working all things for your good, sometimes while here on earth when you are going through a trial, and other times when you get to heaven and view things from My perspective. But I'm telling you in advance—before Chris even takes the tests next Monday—that I am working for your good whatever the outcome is.*

With tears streaming down my face, I could hardly see to drive. A great peace settled over me. Before Chris even took the tests, God was telling me that whatever the results, however good or bad the verdict, He was working it for our good.

Sunday morning, still before Chris's tests, God drew me back to the Hebrews 6 portion once again. At first, I was puzzled that He would keep me devotionally in one portion of Scripture for so long. Then I saw His reason in verse 17:

> In the same way God, desiring even more to show to the heirs of the promise the unchangeableness of His purpose...

I wrote "me" by the word *heirs*. He wanted to show me, an heir of the promise, what? The unchangeableness of His purpose. God was telling me that His purpose for me had not changed since I was twenty-three. He had it all planned from before the foundation of the earth. And just because circumstances changed, which they have over and over again, His purpose for me is still unchangeable.

Chris's test results on Monday did not show that the cancer had spread. Surgery was scheduled and people prayed. I realized through this traumatic experience that God was still working out His purpose in our lives. He was teaching us some eternal values.

Let me share several:

First, *we cannot take answers to prayer for granted.* With a constant flow of answers to multitudes of prayers in our lives, it is easy to take some of them for granted. But watching God work in Chris in answer to prayers from people all over the country has brought a fresh awareness to me of the power of prayer.

HAVING FACED ETERNITY, WE HAVE A NEW SENSE OF COMMITMENT TO WHAT GOD STILL HAS FOR US TO DO.

Second, *we must maintain an "attitude of gratitude."* In my hectic schedule, I had not only taken answers to prayer for granted, I had also let my "attitude of gratitude" slip. Chris and I are now experiencing a continuous, unbelievably deep sense of gratitude to God that Chris's doctor decided to check "a few more things" during a routine exam—and that he found that little lump early enough to get it all. Surgery was 100 percent successful!

I continue to praise God that the cancer was detected before it could spread to any other part of Chris's body. If it had, the outcome would have been completely different.

I stand in awe at how God continues to answer prayer for Chris. His recovery has been truly remarkable with no complications to date.

Third, *we must keep our commitment to Christ fresh.* Having encountered the possibility of facing eternity, Chris and I have a new sense of commitment to what God still has for us to do. The uneasy experience of his retirement has changed to expectancy and thankful waiting upon God for new assignments.

These lessons helped me not only through my husband's bout with cancer, but also gave me strong assurance that God was indeed working out His purpose in my life when I also underwent a cancer test just three weeks after Chris's surgery.

As I lay in bed on the morning of my mammogram, God gently spoke into my heart His time-tested promise in Isaiah 26:3:

> Thou wilt keep him in perfect peace whose mind is stayed on Thee.

Immediately all the tension drained from my body as His peace flooded me. I felt the incredible sense of being completely engulfed in a soft spherical capsule, in the rare atmosphere of God Himself.

As I write this, I haven't received the results of my mammogram.* But God is here. My common sense says, "It's just another exam like all the others." But God is saying, "Before you know the outcome, here is My peace."

There is a word, I have discovered, that transcends all human words, even *cancer*. That word is *God*.

*Editor's note: Evelyn's mammogram showed no signs of cancer.

Sallie Clingman

LESSONS ON
A FIRE ESCAPE

A staff member of Campus Crusade for more than thirty years, Sallie Clingman served with the Christian Embassy in Washington, D.C. where, for many years, she led weekly Bible studies with senate, congressional, and cabinet members' wives. Sallie is now a speaker and consultant to various women's ministries, helping women become more effective ambassadors for Christ.

She also has served as the national women's coordinator for Campus Crusade, spoken at 150 colleges and universities in this country, and traveled in Asia, Africa, and Europe.

She holds a B.S. degree in biology from Centenary College in Louisiana. She also did graduate work in biochemistry at Louisiana State University School of Medicine in New Orleans and worked as a research associate for the university.

Sallie shares her struggle with low self-esteem and the lessons God taught her while sitting on a fire escape at Cam-

pus Crusade headquarters as she prepared to join staff. These lessons helped transform her into a joyful, fruitful servant of the Lord. I know they will encourage your faith as well.

I had never been that lonely in my whole life.

There were 1,251 conferees attending the Institute of Biblical Studies at Arrowhead Springs, at that time the international headquarters for Campus Crusade for Christ. The population for that four-and-a-half-week session consisted primarily of college students and staff of Campus Crusade. I stood out like a sore thumb. I was the "1" of the 1,251.

I had never in my life seen such beautiful people. Every young man looked like the proverbial football hero or president of the student body—or both. Every young woman looked like the head cheerleader or "voted most likely to succeed"—or both. And they were so friendly and cool and comfortable with each other and with God. They prayed for a friend back in Georgia as they stood in line to eat, and they prayed for the professor as they walked to class. They talked to each other freely and talked about Jesus freely. Life seemed natural and easy for them.

I had spent the last six years of my life in a library or a chemistry lab. I was not exactly up on the latest fashions. My social skills were in mothballs, or chloroform, and I was twenty-seven years old. In that crowd I was on the verge of middle age.

I didn't know one other person at the conference. The only one who knew me was Ney Bailey, who at that time was the director of personnel for Campus Crusade. She was from my hometown. Bless her, she took me out to dinner a couple of nights and spoke to me warmly when she saw me.

I was a lonely, out-of-place, miserable misfit. But I knew God wanted me there. My Christian life was new and God had my attention. Only two years earlier, one night in my apartment in New Orleans, I had knelt to invite Jesus Christ to come into my heart. A whole new world had opened up to me and for the first time in my life I knew that I was right with God. I understood that it was not because my good deeds outweighed my bad deeds, but that I had put my faith in Jesus Christ for that "rightness" with God. My assurance was so solid that I desperately wanted to be able to tell other people what I had discovered and what was available to them if they wanted it. That was my motive in going to this conference. Someone had told me that Campus Crusade could teach me to articulate my faith. It was a high priority for me.

Before this trip, someone had commented that my hair had potential but needed some help. So, following their advice, I had colored my hair to—mind you—bring out the "red highlights." Well, my hair looked like an explosion in a Brillo factory—before explosions in Brillo factories were appropriate hair styles.

My twenty-seven-year-old skin looked like thirteen-year-old skin after a chocolate-covered-french-fries frenzy.

My clothes were utterly awful. Lab coats had covered a multitude of fashion sins back in New Orleans, but here I was without my protective layer and I knew I was a disaster.

All of this contributed to the world's worst self-image!

There were about five hundred in my class on the Book of

John. It was a stimulating, thrilling experience for me. However, my loneliness and my misery were so great that I would get to class early to get a seat in the back row near the door so I could escape unnoticed when my next wave of nausea came.

I would have conversations with people and the whole time I was thinking, *All they see is the outside.* They were delightful, caring people, but there was no way they could have known how much I wanted to cry, or how much I envied their apparent lack of pain.

My roommate situation was not any help, either. You could not have assembled four more different people in one room. It was so hot (this was July in Southern California) in our fourth floor, furnaced room that I would climb out onto the fire escape with my pillow to sleep—waiting for a breeze, a stir in the air, a rain shower, anything! One night I was attacked by birds, which only confirmed to me that things were not going to get any better for me at this conference.

We had classes all day. There was the Book of John, New Testament Survey, and Basic Doctrine. At night we heard a series of messages by Dr. Bill Bright. I devoured it all. It's interesting how teachable I get with a little pain. The wisdom I recognized in God's Word was cleansing and my faith was confirmed and encouraged hour after hour. And all the while I carried my fragile emotions from class to class, from meal to meal, and from sleep to sleep.

One night, Dr. Bright spoke from James 1:2–4 and 1 Thessalonians 5:16. He explained that it is an expression of faith or confidence in God to thank Him in trials. This made sense to me. I was certainly getting no relief by *not* thanking God for the discomfort I was having.

I went back to my fourth floor hotbox, climbed out on the fire escape for privacy and cool air, and sat there for what seemed like an eternity—just hurting. The words of James rang in my head. "Consider it all joy, my brethren, when you encounter various trials, knowing that the testing of your faith produces endurance. And let endurance have its perfect result, that you may be perfect and complete, lacking in nothing."

Finally, with a sense of desperate submission to God and His will for my life and character, I leaned my head against the cool iron railing of the fire escape and prayed.

I prayed in a choked whisper punctuated with deep lung-filling and emptying sighs. My prayer was so critical at that point that I remember it word for word:

> God, I want to thank You for all the discomfort I have experienced these weeks. Thank You for the loneliness, thank You for the lousy self-image. You know what You are doing. I trust You.
>
> (Long pause.)
>
> And now I want to tell You that I am willing to have ugly hair, bad skin, to wear unfashionable clothes, and to be alone for the rest of my life—as long as You don't leave me. Amen.

Then my thoughts turned away from me and my pitiful state to the wonder and wisdom of God. My mind raced over the incredible things I had been learning about God in my classes. My heart sensed that God was present and aware of this little person huddled on the fire escape 1,600 miles from home. My lips tried new words of praise and worship to express my new confidence in Him.

There were many lessons to learn from that moment on

the fire escape.

First, my uncomfortable circumstance was not invisible to God.

Second, God's Word, when trusted and obeyed, really changed my life.

Third, God used this rough spot in my life to teach me how subsequent rough spots could be treated.

Fourth, trusting God turned out to be the most important contribution I could make to my own mental and emotional health.

TRUSTING GOD WAS THE MOST IMPORTANT CONTRIBUTION TO MY MENTAL AND EMOTIONAL HEALTH.

Fifth, God changed my life without changing anything about my circumstances.

I came face to face with the character development God was engineering in my life. He was more concerned that my values be right and that my character be Christlike than that I would be comfortable. The great victory for me was that I agreed with God about this and was willing for Him to do what He knew was best.

When I left that conference a week later, I was not asked to be on the cover of *Vogue*, nor was I invited to be on the Johnny Carson Show. I was no Cinderella. But on the inside I was different.

God and I had a secret. We had had an intimate encounter. He had met with me. I knew He had because of the confidence I now had that this was not the last chapter in the story of my life.

I sensed that the conference was a launching pad for

knowing and loving God like I had never dared to dream. I had experienced a glimpse into what really mattered in life. That has prompted me many times in the years since to obey God's Words to "consider it *all* joy."

I had put my faith in God and His Word, and He had worked a miracle in my heart, teaching me that *He is able* to set me free on the inside when there is no escape on the outside.

Sally Conway

LOVE IS STRONGER THAN LIFE'S CIRCUMSTANCES

Sally Conway and her husband, Jim, a former pastor, established a ministry called Mid-Life Dimensions, conducting counseling sessions and seminars for mid-life adults and their families. Together, they touched a nerve in today's fast-paced world.

Sally battled cancer very bravely for several years and maintained a radiant testimony for our Lord before her death in 1998.

Because of her ability to combine wit, understanding, and a firm biblical foundation in a fun and upbeat approach to mid-life crisis, Sally was always in great demand as a speaker. She appeared on local and nationwide radio and TV programs and was considered one of America's foremost family experts.

The mother of three daughters and grandmother of several, Sally authored many books and was an adjunct professor at Talbot Theological Seminary for five years.

Bill and I met the Conways many years ago, before midlife crisis for men was even a consideration. I am not aware that my husband has had one, or that every man does, but Sally shares insight into how to cope with the situation.

My husband angrily grabbed his coat and slammed out the door. My heart sank to my feet where it had been so often lately. I thought we had been doing better recently. Yes, he still seemed depressed and confused much of the time, but generally he didn't blame me so much anymore.

As I watched Jim walk away down the snowy drive, I realized I had been off guard this evening. I had nagged a little bit here and there and had even questioned an insignificant decision he'd made. Until a few months ago he would have let those careless remarks go unchallenged. He was the one with the wide shoulders and the uncritical spirit. But now he had become hypersensitive, and I had to measure my words and reactions carefully. At times he would partially come out of his depression and be stronger emotionally, and then the slightest thing would trigger his anger and another down cycle.

I knew how much he hated the snow and cold, and since he wasn't adequately dressed, I didn't expect him to stay out long. Besides, this was the night before Thanksgiving and one of our daughters had arrived home from college only minutes before. We were planning a special welcome-home supper.

But Jim didn't return in time to eat with the family. We have a strong family tradition of waiting for everyone to gather before we eat. But each of the girls had other, previously arranged commitments, so they finally nibbled on something and went their ways. This kind of situation had never occurred before in our family. The special meal and I waited. I reset the table for two with special placemats and candles.

Eventually Jim did come home. He accepted my apology and seemed amiable as we ate our meal together by candlelight. Little did I know how much was still raging within him—some anger toward me, but mostly confusion and terror from the deeper struggles he couldn't understand within himself. We went to bed, and he spent the night in a furious battle with himself and God that I didn't know about until morning. I didn't know at the time how close that came to being our last night together in our bed.

Jim was in the throes of a gigantic mid-life crisis that lasted more than three years. He wanted to run from all his responsibilities. He was depressed. He swung back and forth between being sullen and fomenting with anger.

He declared that he had lost all feelings for me. In fact, he said, "I've never really loved you. It was a mistake for us to have married."

This was so unlike the optimistic, loving, Christ-centered man with whom I had already spent over twenty-three years of life and ministry. His perception about his world was totally off balance.

During the days that became weeks, months, and years of Jim's turmoil, I kept remembering a scene from my childhood. Part of the backbone I needed to enable me to help my husband through his mid-life crisis was provided by that earlier experience.

My family and I were heartsick! A hailstorm had just demolished our expected income. My mother stood beside me outside our small, white farmhouse after the devastating summer storm had passed. We leaned on the rain-dampened fence that separated our little yard of grass and flowers from the rest of the farmyard. Our house was on a hill with barns and pens of dairy cows, pigs, sheep, and chickens situated here and there down the hillside.

We were looking across a small valley to the next hill where our corn crop had just been shredded by hail. A big portion of our year's income lay pounded into a sickening mass on the ground over on that hill.

I knew Mother grieved over the work and expense that had gone into that cornfield. This was about 1944 and my parents hadn't completely recovered from the Great Depression. Nebraska farmers were never too far from disaster anyway. Within a few moments, hail or windstorms could completely wipe out all hopes of catching up with past years' deficits. If it wasn't the weather, it might be insects or diseases or a drop in grain and livestock prices.

Mother and Daddy had been married about twelve years before they felt they could afford to buy their own farm. On the day this hailstorm hit, they still owed a large debt. We needed every crop, each animal, the eggs, and cream from our dairy cows to pay for our farm and to cover our other expenses. Sometimes the success or failure of just one of these income sources determined whether or not we would lose the farm.

That day as we viewed our ruined crop, Mother probably said something about her fears and the wasted work and money. I don't remember. What I do remember is her arm around my shoulder and her words, "You know, honey, a husband and wife can take anything that comes in life as long as they love each other."

In the years that followed, my parents were good models of a loving couple who can "take anything." That tough bond lasted until Daddy's death at age eighty-three, and Mother still carries her part to this day.

I am a long way from that little farm now, which, by the way, we were able to keep in spite of many more storms and losses. I grew up there, graduated from high school, went away to college, and came back to be married in the little church in our nearest town.

I married a man who was called into Christian ministry. Jim and I went off to seminary as newlyweds. Over a period of thirty years we pastored part-time student churches and three full-time churches. We learned so much as we hurt with our people when they hurt and rejoiced when they rejoiced. During that time God gave us three daughters to nurture. They are now grown, married, launched into people-helping pursuits, and raising children of their own.

A few years ago, God moved Jim and me from a local church ministry to teaching in a seminary and pastoring the nation's hurting mid-life couples. We know firsthand what mid-lifers experience.

My own mid-life crisis a few years before Jim's was one of the first hard tests that directly affected our marriage. I went through a great deal of confusion, feeling unneeded and unappreciated, while Jim was busy with his important work of "winning the world."

Jim wisely saw that I needed to establish my own identity and sense of value. He knew I enjoyed being a pastor's wife and mother, but he encouraged me to combine those callings with going back to school and finding a ministry within our church that fit my God-given talents. His committed love helped me balance my life so I could once again "bloom where I was planted."

Trials to test our marriage bond have also come in other ways. For years our family experienced a wide gamut of physical problems—surgeries, broken bones, stitches, life-threatening reactions to bee stings, four out of five of us having mononucleosis, and the list goes on.

One fall while our daughter Brenda was still recovering from mono, she was hospitalized in her college health center with a viral infection. Her older sister, Barbara, was brought into the center with a severely fractured collar bone from a bike accident. As Brenda got out of bed to go comfort Barbara, she fainted and hit her head; she was taken to a city hospital where X-rays revealed a concussion.

Leaving Jim at home in the worst trough of his mid-life crisis, I drove to the college and eventually brought Barbara home because she couldn't use either arm. We didn't know at the time that in spite of an upper-body cast and several kinds of treatments, her collar bone would not heal for over a year.

We simply went on to the next health problem that fall. In a few days our youngest daughter, Becki, was to have a second biopsy of a tumor in her left leg. By spring the lab test results and many experts' opinions concluded that her tumor was a rare malignancy that required drastic action. Tragically, her leg had to be amputated above mid-thigh.

Jim had thoroughly believed that God would heal Becki's leg. When the miracle didn't come through, he nearly went off the deep end completely. "When Becki lost her leg, I lost God!" he cried many times later. I stood by him as he wrestled with why God would allow such a thing to happen to his vivacious sixteen-year-old daughter. He eventually arrived at a place of peace where he could "let God be God."

Other strains in our lives have included two times in the last few years when we have felt that God was leading us into a certain direction in our ministry and both ended in failure. Failure is an awful word, and it took me a long time to be able to say it in regard to our plans.

LOVE MEANS WE VALUE THE OTHER, EVEN WHEN THAT ONE IS NOT LOVING IN RETURN.

In both cases we went into personal debt for thousands of dollars. In fact, every time I look at our threadbare, outdated living room furniture, I am reminded that we could have had a nicely decorated house for ourselves and furniture for a lot of other people, too, if we hadn't lost that money in what we thought was God's will for our ministry. Worse than the financial loss, though, was the loss of esteem we each felt from having to withdraw from these projects.

Probably the most difficult path we have had to walk, however, has come in recent years. Quite unexpectedly, Jim has begun a journey of recalling his troubled childhood. Actually, now that he is able to bring it to the surface, the going is easier than it was.

While all the boyhood pain and neglect have been bubbling out, we have both had to call on every ounce of devotion we had for each other. Sometimes I have been mistaken for the unfair, judgmental authority figure that squelched his personhood as a boy. He has reacted like the hurt little four-year-old, the selfish seven-year-old, or the sassy ten-year-old that he never got to be at those ages.

Jim has agonized over the realization that for decades he had buried the awful secret of his dysfunctional family, a secret that has extended its ugly tentacles in many directions with sad consequences for innocent people. Once he could face the truth about his family, he began to find freedom from his shame. It has not been easy, however.

As we face our own places of pain and as we work with mid-life couples whose long-term marriages are breaking or nearly broken, I keep hearing my mother's words, "A husband and wife can take anything that comes in life as long as they love each other."

Together Jim and I have learned that if a husband and wife love each other, they *are* able to "take everything" that happens in life. We've also learned that love is not simply a feeling. Love isn't over when the feelings aren't there. Lasting love is not something we fall into and out of.

Love is a commitment, a determination to contribute all that we can to the building of something beautiful and satisfying for both of us. Love means we value the other, even when that one is not loving in return. In spite of all the hurts and bashings that life can give, a marriage relationship can last.

Many people have taught me lots of valuable lessons—by word and by example. But the greatest lesson I learned has been used day in and day out for thirty-six years of my marriage and as Jim and I work to help other marriages survive. How innocently it took place that evening when Mother pointed out that love in a marriage relationship is stronger than life's circumstances.[1]

Joy Dawson

WHAT IT MEANS TO FEAR THE LORD

Joy Dawson has been traveling and teaching the Bible internationally since 1970, mostly at spiritual leadership conferences. A woman with a world vision, her missionary journeys have taken her to fifty-five nations spanning every continent. She has taught extensively on television and radio, and countless lives have been eternally touched through the worldwide distribution of her books and audio and video tapes. The character and ways of God are the biblical basis of her penetrating teachings. She is author of numerous books, including Intimate Friendship with God.

A woman of prayer, Joy is vivacious and "wound tight" to make her small in stature but tall in word and deed. It was a pleasure to work with her as a member of the National Day of Prayer Committee.

Joy has been a great encouragement to me. Ask her counsel and you will always receive a biblical answer. The Scrip-

tures are her authority, as you will see from what she shares in this lesson.

By the time I was a young wife and mother, I was painfully aware of my lack of wisdom. Consequently, I tried several ways to remedy this weakness in my character.

One was to listen to what wise people said, hoping to gather up their pearls of wisdom and then use them at the appropriate moments when conversing with others. But for some inexplicable reasons, I never seemed to successfully match the pearls with the right moments!

Then I observed that the people whom I considered wise were mostly silent. So I tried that tactic and found the frustration wasn't worth the effort. The family from which I came were all strongly opinionated and had a lot to say. I didn't seem to fit the silent mold. All too frequently I had to humble myself and ask forgiveness for having said the wrong thing.

Wisdom, it seemed, just wasn't my thing.

There were other areas in my life where I found it difficult to make necessary changes. Although I would confess my sins to God, I would not always get to the place of real repentance.

All of this troubled me because I had a deep and sincere desire for intimate friendship with God. But I had no workable solutions—*until* the Holy Spirit sovereignly drew my attention to the many verses in the Bible on the subject of *the fear of the Lord.* What a gold mine of truth I discovered. Let me share some of the lessons I learned.

First, "The fear of the Lord is to *hate* evil" (Proverbs 8:13). That means having God's attitude toward sin at all times. If I hated sin, it would be easy for me to choose not to sin. I would not do the things I hated unless forced to by a higher authority. This brought me to conclude that the reason I had chosen to sin was because I had a love for that sin in my heart. The love for the sin needed to be replaced with a hatred for it. *The fear of the Lord* would give me that hatred.

This simple but profound truth was reinforced by finding Proverbs 16:6: "Through the fear of the Lord a man *avoids* evil." What an incredible discovery this became to me. The reason I was not repenting of the sins I had so often confessed was because I lacked the fear of the Lord.

Day after day as I read the Word of God, I would write down more verses on the subject in a big notebook I titled *The Character and the Ways of God*. It was my personal concordance of verses which related to that title from my devotional readings. The more I meditated on what I wrote down on *the fear of the Lord* (which amounted to sixty-six verses), the more I realized that it was the answer to every area of weakness in my character.

Second, "The fear of the Lord is the *beginning* of wisdom" and "the *beginning* of knowledge" (Proverbs 9:10; 1:7). In Job 28:12, Job asked, "Where can wisdom be found? Where does understanding dwell?" I certainly could identify with that question. Obviously he understood my inquiry at a deep level.

No amount of wealth, Job said, can purchase wisdom or be compared with its value. It is hidden from man's understanding, but "God understands the way to it and he alone knows where it dwells" (Job 28:23). Then came a brilliant burst of truth: "And he [God] said to man, 'The fear of the Lord—that is wisdom, and to shun evil is understanding'" (Job 28:28).

I decided to make an in-depth study of *the fear of the Lord* and apply it to every area of my life.

I was encouraged to know that at least I was *beginning* to act upon a truth that would revolutionize my life more than any other.

Third, "The fear of the Lord is the *instruction* of wisdom" (Proverbs 15:33). I saw that I could have as much wisdom as I chose to be holy. The light bulbs of truth were being switched on in my mind and spirit. What release to submit to the Person of the Holy Spirit to work this in me and then through me to others.

From then on I repeatedly asked God for *the fear of the Lord* and received it by faith. The change in my life was as perceptible as a butterfly coming out of a chrysalis. The truth was setting me free. Not only did I experience a whole new hatred of sin in thought, word, and deed, but God's wisdom began to replace my human wisdom which at its best was embarrassing!

Fourth, "Come, my children, listen to me; I will *teach* you the fear of the Lord" (Psalm 34:11). I continued to write out each verse on *the fear of the Lord* as it appeared in my daily Bible reading and to meditate on each aspect of this truth. This led to the further discovery of God's special school on this subject as recorded in Psalm 34:11–13.

I pictured myself as a small child in a kindergarten, sitting on my little chair along with others in God's family, being taught by my fascinating teacher, God. It was a cozy scene and I was excited to learn.

How interesting to find that the first lesson in my kindergarten related to the discipline of the tongue (v. 13). I would learn that we can soon tell to what degree people fear the Lord by just listening to what they say—or just as important, what they don't say.

I pondered deeply at the high standard God set in His Word about 100 percent honesty, 100 percent of the time: "Keep your lips from speaking deceit" (Psalm 34:13). I realized there would have to be changes—no overstating, no understating, no misquoting someone by reporting what he or she said out of context. I started to think about the many times I had said, "I'd love to, but…" when declining invitations to do things or go places, when I didn't really want to be involved at all. Unless I really did want to, I learned to eliminate the words "I'd love to."

WHEN SIN HOLDS NO FASCINATION FOR US, WE NEED NOT FEAR THE STRONGEST TEMPTATIONS.

I thought about the times I had believed that as long as I said some facts that were truthful about a given situation, *that* was speaking the truth. The more I pursued *the fear of the Lord,* the more I realized that the truth is stated only when we have given enough facts to convey truth.

Fifth, *the fear of the Lord* is the only way to be released from the fear of man, which Proverbs 29:25 says will prove to be a snare. I had experienced the bondage that comes from being more impressed with man's reactions to my actions than with God's reaction.

The more God-conscious I became, the less self-conscious I was. The more concern I had for God's approval in every situation, the more confidence He released in me to act with His authority. *The fear of the Lord* brought freedom.

Sixth, it was wonderful to discover that when sin holds no fascination for us because we hate it, we need not fear the strongest or the most subtle temptations. Isaiah prophesied that when Jesus came He would "delight in the fear of the Lord." To me this suggests experiencing the joyous freedom that comes from living a holy life in thought, word, and deed. Free to be natural, open, loving, and honest with nothing to hide.

Although there was a lot to learn, it was not complicated. To obtain *the fear of the Lord* and maintain it, I discovered, I must desire it deeply, continually ask God for it and receive it by faith, keep studying the subject from His Word, and act upon the truth He reveals.

Living in *the fear of the Lord* not only became a liberating way of life but an exciting adventure.

Judy Douglass

SEARCHING FOR SIGNIFICANCE

A Campus Crusade for Christ staff member for more than thirty-five years, Judy Douglass served as editor of Collegiate Challenge *and* Worldwide Challenge *magazines and director of the publications department. She is currently a consulting editor for* Worldwide Challenge, *a freelance writer, and the author of three books that address issues facing singles and young mothers.*

Judy assists her husband, Steve, in leading the U.S. Ministries of Campus Crusade. She is a frequent speaker at college campus and church women's groups, retreats, missions conferences, and singles gatherings. She also has taught at writers' workshops.

She and her husband have two daughters. When her first child was born, Judy went home to "be a mom" and found that transition one of the more challenging adjustments of her life. You will be blessed as Judy describes her search for significance and how she discovered it.

My daughters, Debbie and Michelle, placed the array of angels on our table—two bright silver ones, a shiny brass angel, a lovely ceramic bell—while Steve lighted the elegant angel candle. I dished up peach cobbler for each of us. We were preparing to "celebrate with the angels."

"Yesterday Mom spoke to a group of women about Jesus," my husband, Steve, began. "Three of them said they wanted to invite Jesus into their lives as their Savior."

"You had a part in those women receiving Christ," I reminded the girls, "because you allowed me to go and share with them and because you prayed that God would use me in a special way. Now there are three new children in the family of God."

"What are the angels doing?" Steve asked.

"They're having a party!" Michelle exclaimed.

"They're celebrating because people asked Jesus into their hearts!" Debbie added.

All four of us prayed, thanking God for the privilege of helping introduce people to Christ, thanking Him for these new sisters in the Lord, and praying for them as they began their new lives in Christ. Then we ate our cobbler.

The "celebrate with the angels" party has become a cherished tradition in our home every time one of us is involved in the birth of a new believer. Every time we do that, God reminds us of the incredible privilege it is to tell people about His love. At those times I feel very significant. I feel that every little thing I do is important.

But I don't always feel that way. I particularly remember a conference one summer evening several years ago.

"The hour is urgent," the speaker was saying. "The world needs the Lord Jesus Christ. The world is hungry for God. This is no time for business as usual. Our lives must be supernatural. We must be spiritual revolutionaries."

"Sure," I thought to myself. "When will I ever do anything significant for the Lord again?"

Certainly I had achieved some significant accomplishments. At eight years of age I had decided I wanted to become a writer. When I received Christ at the age of fifteen, I had a definite sense that God had something special He wanted me to do. How thrilled I was that what He wanted me to do was write and edit for Him.

For fourteen years I had the privilege of working in the publications department of Campus Crusade for Christ, writing and editing—to touch lives for Christ. I had seen God do wonderful things in my life and through my life. I felt very much as though I were living a supernatural life, as though I were making a significant contribution to the cause of Christ.

But now I had a very active fourteen-month-old. Just maintaining daily life overwhelmed me. And I was pregnant. When would I ever find the time to reach out and minister to even one other person, much less do anything truly significant or satisfying?

My diminished sense of significance or self-worth shouldn't have been a surprise. Rather, it's a common response to the demands of mothering. But knowing that didn't lessen my frustration or simplify my search.

Psychologist Bruce Narramore tells us that most psychologists agree on which basic conditions in life contribute to our sense of significance or value. Five of the most important criteria for personal worth and significance are security, confidence, a sense of belonging, a feeling of being loved, and a sense of purpose.

In my career I had experienced personal worth in all of these areas. I felt secure in my job, primarily because I was sure I was doing what God had called me to do.

I had confidence. I had been doing my work long enough to know I was doing a good job and was comfortable with it.

I definitely had a sense of belonging. My co-workers and I were very close and had an excellent working relationship.

I felt loved by those I worked with as well as by my husband and other important people in my life.

And the assurance that my writing and editing touched lives for the Lord gave a tremendous purpose to my life.

My new role of motherhood, however, gave me little assurance of value in any of these areas.

Security. I did feel secure in this job. There was no one else to do it, though there were times I felt like giving the responsibility to someone else. I often did not feel sure of my health or my sanity. And my "just surviving" mentality hardly gave me a sense of real security.

Confidence. I did not find mothering easy and I had almost no confidence that I was doing an adequate job. I read a lot of books, and sometimes they helped, but too often they caused me to feel that I was inferior or a failure.

Belonging. Yes, there was a sense that I belonged to this child. But I had little opportunity to belong anywhere else. I often missed the camaraderie of the office.

Being loved. I was still certain of my husband's love, though I didn't feel lovely very often. As for my wonderful little daughter, she generally made demands rather than returning love to me.

Purpose. I knew that what I was doing in Debbie's life had great, long-term significance and purpose. But because there was little tangible evidence of results in those early days, it was hard to recognize any purpose.

Fortunately, God did not leave me hanging in frustration and insignificance. Nor did He allow me to shut myself away from the significant opportunities He had for me. Through study of His Word, extensive conversations with my husband, and the counsel of godly mothers, God provided His perspective on my life as a mother.

First, He dealt with my lost sense of significance. He reminded me that He, and He alone, was the source of my personal value and worth.

He reminded me that He loved me unconditionally (Romans 5:8), eternally (Jeremiah 31:3), and sacrificially (John 15:13).

He made me aware that my security had to be in Him, and that in Him I was truly safe. Jesus said, "No one can snatch them [my sheep] out of my hand" (John 10:28).

He reminded me that in Him—and only in Him—I can have confidence. I am a special person, created in God's image (Genesis 1:26,27). I am the crown of creation (Psalm 8:4,5). I am capable of great accomplishments (Philippians 4:13). God is my source of and reason for confidence.

God reminded me that I belong in the greatest group of all—His own family. He adopted me and made me His own child (Ephesians 1:4–6; John 1:12).

Then He showed me that I have a significant purpose.

His primary purpose in my life is to make me like Jesus (Romans 8:28,29). As I become more and more like Christ, I will fulfill His purpose for me by reflecting the glory of God (1 Peter 2:9).

God has other specific purposes for my life as well. One is to bear good fruit: "You did not choose Me, but I chose you, and appointed you, that you should go and bear fruit, and that your fruit should remain" (John 15:16). Also, God has prepared good works for me: "For we are God's workmanship, created in Christ Jesus to do good works, which God prepared in advance for us to do" (Ephesians 2:10). In the parable of the talents (Matthew 25:14–30), Christ tells us that we are to be good stewards of all that He gives us in life.

GOD REMINDED ME THAT HE, AND HE ALONE, WAS THE SOURCE OF MY PERSONAL VALUE AND WORTH.

As I understood that all I have is because I have Jesus, I began to recognize that it was not meeting all these important criteria in my life—in my career and ministry, or as a mother— that brought fulfillment. Rather it arose

out of my relationship with God through Jesus Christ. He alone could give me the love, security, confidence, sense of belonging, and purpose for my life that I needed.

Thus, over time, God restored my sense of significance, unrelated to my mothering or any ministry I might have. He provided for my need for significance.

And then, when I clearly understood the true source of my significance, He began increasingly to unfold for me the significant opportunities He had for me. I gained a strong vision for the incredibly important—and significant—job I had as a mother. And step by step He led me into creative ways of touching lives for Him—ways that fit me, my abilities, and the needs of my family.

When I focus on Christ, He fills me with a true sense of significance. And that frees me to do the significant works He has planned for me.

Colleen Townsend Evans

LEARNING TO SAY NO

Colleen Evans served for 16 years on the board of directors of World Vision, U.S., and is a board member of Presbyterians for Renewal. She is on the advisory boards of International Justice Mission, a Christian witness for justice around the world, and Women at the Well, a ministry for women.

Colleen and her husband, Louis, are partners in renewal ministries, which involve men's/women's retreats, pastor/spouse retreats, and marriage and family conferences, as well as efforts aimed at improving cross-cultural relationships, and other ministries.

In 1987 she was named "Churchwoman of the Year" by Religious Heritage of America. She has received honorary doctorates from New York's King's College and Eastern College in St. David's, Pennsylvania.

After playing parts in several movies in the 1940s, "Coke" (as she is known to her closest friends) set aside a promising film career to marry Louis H. Evans, Jr. in 1950.

The first years of their marriage were spent at San Francisco Theological Seminary, followed by two years at New College, University of Edinburgh, Scotland. She and her husband served the Bel Air Presbyterian Church and the La Jolla Presbyterian Church in California, and the National Presbyterian Church in Washington, D.C. They are now back in California at Menlo Park Presbyterian Church.

The Evanses have three sons and a daughter, and nine grandchildren.

Colleen is the author of nine books and with her husband is the co-author of a book on marriage.

When I asked Colleen to share the "greatest lesson" in her life, she thought of the many important things she has discovered over the years. What you are about to read was perhaps not her greatest lesson, but it certainly was one of the most practical. Had she not learned it, she most likely would not have been here to respond to my request. Here is her story.

It all began in the late 1950s. So much in my life was new then: I was a relatively new Christian; I became a new wife—then a new mother—and finally, when my husband finished seminary and graduate school, we were called to start a new church.

It was heady wine for someone who had always loved people and had a deep desire to serve. But to be honest, that was not the whole picture. I also wanted to please people and to have them care about me in return.

The new church that Louie, my husband, had been asked

to start was in Bel Air, an area in the hills above Los Angeles. It was an exciting new challenge for us, and we both dived in with energy and enthusiasm.

The church had nowhere to meet except in the living room of our low, gray, California-style frame house on Roscomare Road. This didn't present a problem for me—at first. We kept 150 folding chairs (our first furniture, other than beds!) in the garage for our constant stream of meetings and used the front bedroom for a church office.

After awhile, the growing congregation was able to rent the local elementary school auditorium for Sunday worship, but all the other meetings continued to be held in our home. It was almost a full-time job—setting up chairs, greeting people, taking down chairs, keeping the house in order, baking cookies, making punch, keeping the coffee pot on for meetings and drop-in callers at all times of the day and night.

In addition to all the church activities in our home, I also felt compelled to be involved in things outside our home. A community activist by nature, I seemed constitutionally unable to turn down requests to serve worthwhile causes. So I became chairperson for the Beverly Hills Bel Air Community Chest drive—which, looking back, was insane for me to chair during that season of my life.

By this time, I was no longer a "new" mother. We now had four babies, all under the age of five. It seemed that I could never quite finish folding one load of clean diapers before it was time to begin another.

After a church meeting one night, when the last lingering parishioner had headed home, I dragged myself to our bedroom and fell into bed utterly exhausted. The rest felt unbelievably good, but it was short-lived. A stirring from the cradle put me on notice that our youngest was ready for his midnight feeding. Almost automatically, I stumbled out of bed, picked him up, sat down in my rocker and began to nurse him. It was then that I looked over at Louie sleeping soundly.

The light of a full moon streamed through a crack between our draperies, looking like an eerie iridescent spotlight focused on the handsome face of my husband. He looked *so* comfortable, *so* rested, *so* like a Greek god in repose. And I felt a sudden flood of envy. No, more than envy: resentment, tinged with anger. Why couldn't he be more help, especially in the middle of the night?

Well, of course, I knew he couldn't nurse the baby. But at that moment I was in no mood to be logical. I was angry and I was tired and I had to blame somebody for something.

My attitude at that moment did not honor God, but it was honest (and God honors our honesty). It also served a purpose, for it let me know that I was in trouble and needed help. That fact was confirmed when I went to see my doctor, who also was a close family friend, for a checkup a few days later.

"To be frank, I'm really tired," I told him when he asked how I'd been feeling.

"No wonder!" he exclaimed, reading the lab report in front of him. "You're really anemic. I should put you in the hospital to see if we can build you up a bit."

"But Frosty," I sputtered to our longtime friend, "who would take care of Louie and the children, cook for the two prayer breakfasts each week, keep our home ready for all the church meetings, take over my responsibilities with the Community Chest fund drive, and…?"

I was about to run out of breath. "Frosty, you just *can't*

put me in the hospital!"

He just sat there shaking his head. "Do you have any household help?"

I laughed. "Help? On a new church development salary? No way!"

If I expected sympathy from my good friend, I was dead wrong. He looked at me with his intensely blue eyes, and without a tinge of "There, there," let me have it.

"Coke, you're crazy. Absolutely crazy. You're trying to be superwife, supermom, superfriend to everyone. And the truth is, you're becoming a supermartyr who doesn't know how to take care of herself. I know how much you want to serve the Lord and the whole world, but if you keep this up, you won't be able to serve anybody.

"Four babies—all that church stuff—and you still say yes to everybody who asks you to do anything. If you don't learn how to say *no*—and fast—you'll be burned out before you're thirty-five!"

I was stunned. His no-nonsense lecture got through to me. I knew that if I didn't make some immediate changes in my life, Frosty would be forced to make them for me.

As I left his office and drove home through the heavy Los Angeles traffic, I felt depressed. I feared Louie would be disappointed in me when I told him things were going to have to change, that I was going to have to cut back. But I was wrong.

Louie was wonderfully supportive, and this gave me a ray of insight. *He* was not the one pushing me to do so many things; *I* was. It wasn't Louie or the Lord driving me into an unhealthy lifestyle. It was my own expectations for myself. What Louie *really* wanted was for me to be the person God created me to be, and to enjoy him and the children. And so I began to relax—and pray in earnest.

"God, guide me. Show me how to live. Tell me what I must cut out of my schedule. Lord, please, with all of my heart, I want *You* to become the Lord of my daily routine."

HAVING NURTURED

OUR RELATIONSHIPS

AT HOME, WE

COULD REACH

OUT TO A BROKEN

WORLD FROM

A SOLID BASE.

I confess there were moments when I thought, *Maybe God will send me a maid. Most of my neighbors have maids and I need help as much as they do.* But God's wisdom prevailed, and that never happened. If God had supplied a maid, I would have continued in the disobedience of an unhealthy schedule. And Christ would never have been allowed to control the comings and goings of my life.

Instead, God continued to give me needed insight into myself. My priorities were wrong. For this season of my life, I was not to be out saving the world. There would be time for that later. But for now, I was to stay at home to care for my family and for

myself. Most of all, I was to concentrate on nurturing my relationship with Christ, with my very special partner in life, and with the four tiny, beautiful human beings with whom God was trusting us for a brief time.

With radical clarity, God revealed to me that Louie and I could not continue ministering to needy people until we learned to minister in Christ's name to one another. Then, having nurtured our relationships at home, we could reach out to a broken world from a solid base.

So it wasn't a maid I needed. It was a realigning of priorities, a judicious pruning of activities. But that was not as easily done as said, for it meant giving up my dream of trying to please everybody. It meant making some people angry as I turned down their telephone requests, or sent out polite but firm notes of resignation. It was tough, but my mind was made up. In my new way of thinking, it had to be God's opinion that mattered most—and it had to be Christ, *not other people*, who ruled my life.

Consequently, I learned the lesson Frosty said I must learn to survive. And I began to say no to a lot of very good things—good, but not God's best for that season of my life. At the same time, I learned to say yes to people who had been wanting to help me with all sorts of things. And that opened the door to let some very gracious people into my life.

In the months that followed, when someone asked me to take on a responsibility I believed was not God's best, I felt increasingly free to say, "Thanks for thinking of me, but this isn't the time for that kind of involvement."

I was in the process of being liberated from my terrible need to be superwoman. I discovered that I didn't feel guilty for turning people down. I was able to stop condemning myself and chomping at the bit because of the limitations of my strength and circumstances. God was doing a real and much-needed work in me, and I was experiencing a joy and satisfaction in my daily life that I hadn't known in years. There is no question that learning to say no was a turning point in my life.

Now, many years later, the joy remains. Indeed, it has grown. And I am so deeply grateful to God for teaching me the importance of learning to say no through that painful experience. It is a lesson that has served me well. And amazingly, some of the very things I had to say no to in earlier seasons have returned as opportunities for a new season in my life.

If you are caught, as I was, in the barrenness of a too-busy life, look to Jesus. The Gospels reveal Him as a man who had learned the importance of saying no. There were times when He said no to the demands and requests made of Him, times when He said no to the crowd and got away to be alone with His disciples, times when He left the disciples to be alone with His Father.

Jesus looked to God for guidance and direction for His days. He listened for that one voice over the roar of all other voices calling for His time and energy and help. And so must we. For Jesus that meant that sometimes He did not get to those close to Him in their time of need. He did not get to His cousin John in prison before Herod took off his head, nor did He heed the call of Mary and Martha to be with Lazarus as he lay ill and dying. (And can't you just see Martha pacing the floor and muttering, "Where's that Jesus when we need Him most?")

And so we, like Jesus, must listen for that one voice above every other, and let God guide us in every aspect of our daily lives. But that will mean learning the important lesson of being willing to say *no* to people in order to say *yes* to God.

Then, and only then, will our great and loving Lord be able to reveal His greater plan through us, as He did to Mary and Martha in the resurrection of Lazarus.

Mary Graham

A LONGING TO
BE ACCEPTED

Mary Graham is president of Women of Faith, *a ministry that hosts conferences for women throughout the country.*

A native of Oklahoma, Mary earned a sociology degree from California State University in Fresno. Motivated by a desire to work with students, she joined the Campus Crusade for Christ staff in 1969, and has served the Lord at the Universities of New Mexico, Kansas, and Utah.

Mary worked for three years as Director of International Ministries with Insight for Living, *Dr. Charles Swindoll's radio ministry. She currently serves on its board of directors. Mary also was the executive producer and director of* Women Today With Vonette Bright, *a daily radio program.*

Being the youngest in a family of eight children has profoundly affected her life, giving her wisdom, humor, and insight that make her one of the most delightful and spiritually mature persons I have known.

"Little House on the Prairie" it was not. Yet, in many ways, growing up in our home in Picher, Oklahoma, was almost as ideal: a little house, a small community, and a loving family. The children were taught strong moral values, fierce family loyalty, and a commitment to the work ethic and the American way.

My father expressed his philosophy of child-rearing in these terms: "Tell them they can't do something and they will prove to you they can," and, "Never tell them they did well or they won't try to do better." There was no question about his heart's desire. He wanted his children to be hardworking, high-achieving, and well-accomplished adults who made positive contributions to life.

My mother's philosophy was equally demanding. She said it simply: "Stay out of trouble."

So often I recall their challenge to me, "Be something." And, "Behave."

Success in life was thus well-defined and I thought easily attained. But being the youngest of eight children, I had too many sidewalk captains giving me orders. Nothing was easy.

My parents had four girls, then three boys, then me. They described it like this: "First we had the girls, then we had the boys, then we had Mary." The female side of the family was always referred to as "the girls and Mary."

I'll never forget the day I phoned home and my dad answered, "Hi, honey." I could hear Mother in the background, "Is that one of the girls?" Without a second thought he answered, "No, it's Mary. You want to talk to her?"

The "girls" were all teenagers by the time I learned to walk and talk. They were not interested in my being one of them, and the boys—a small band of terrorists looking for someone to attack—were not interested in having their baby sister among their ranks either. That didn't diminish my popularity, unfortunately, as the candidate for their numerous shenanigans.

During those growing-up years, my heart longed to be wanted. I tried everything to fill this need. I pestered everyone. In an effort to appease me, Mother forced the boys to include me in their games—unless I cried. Countless times I heard her say, "I cannot make them play with you if you cry." Thus they learned quickly that getting rid of me was simple: Make her cry. If tears stunted growth, I'd be about an inch tall.

The boys were dreadful. They entertained themselves, and each other, with whatever was close at hand—like walking on old oil drums. As they balanced themselves on those big barrels and danced their little feet backwards and forwards, they looked like circus clowns. So agile. So gifted. So enviable. I wanted to do that.

"Never!" they declared. "Girls can't do this. You have to do two things at once, balance yourself and walk. Girls can only do one thing at a time—one or the other. Never both."

"Why?" I asked.

"Because they're girls," they insisted.

But I didn't give up. Finally, one of the boys responded to my persistent plea. "Okay, here's what you can do. Take the barrel up the hill. Get on it and balance yourself. That's all. Just one thing. The barrel will move down the hill on its own; you will not need to walk. It will roll itself."

Great! I thought. Well, not quite great. The barrel rolled on its own all right. It threw me off, then ran over me. I cried. My brothers were in complete unsympathetic hysterics.

"Girls!" they muttered. "Hmpf!"

Although the boys were mean to me, it was easy to see that they liked each other. My sisters liked each other, too. Clearly, the boys and the girls were friends, comrades, teams —at least with each other. So, to be included, I resolved to be like them.

Whatever they did, I did. Or at least tried. Life became adventuresome, albeit tiring. My energies were extremely focused: Perform. Their edict, my marching orders.

And so it went throughout my life. I earned a master's degree in the "performing arts." I learned to please people—my parents, my siblings, my teachers, peers, friends— everybody. I performed and lived on their agendas. It worked well for me. I looked and felt successful.

My theme in life could have been summed up in four words: "I can do that." Wherever I went, whatever need I perceived, no matter the cost, my response was always the same: "Oh, I can do that. No problem."

As a high school student, I was on the debate team. My partner, Bob, was clearly one of the best, most highly acclaimed debaters in the state. He was two years my senior and far outdistanced me in ability and experience. It was an honor to be on his team.

Anyone with as little experience as I was crazy to compete in his league. Not I. I was so accustomed to reaching beyond my own limitations, so attuned to trying harder and reaching higher that I rose to the challenge.

Although I was over my head by anyone's standard, this didn't stop me. I said whatever was necessary to win. I performed well, and we won. It was as simple as that. I knew no other way. The anxiety and stress I felt was at times tremendous, but never overwhelming. Such experiences defined and amplified my entire life.

Then I gave my heart to Christ.

As a junior in college, I discovered His love for me and received His forgiveness. I trusted Him to take absolute and irrevocable control of my life. My heart's desire was to please and honor Him. I learned that the only way to do that was "by faith."

Those who discipled me as a new believer were careful to instruct me in that faith. They consistently taught and modeled the biblical perspective: "God is not as concerned with your performance as He is with the attitude of your heart. He's not as interested in what you do as who you are inside." This was diametrically opposed to every standard I had ever known.

GOD IS NOT AS INTERESTED IN WHAT YOU DO AS WHO YOU ARE INSIDE.

With all of my being, I wanted to believe these truths. I wanted to understand God's grace. I wanted to experience His

unconditional love for me. I wanted to believe His promise in John 15:9, "Just as the Father has loved Me, I have also loved you." And in Romans 15:7, "I have accepted you." And in Matthew 6:33, "I will care for you."

In my mind, I grasped the truth of these promises and clung as tightly as possible to their reliability. But somehow I could not always make them work in my life. They needed to go deeper into the foundation of my soul, to find solid ground. I needed an emotional framework to turn theory into practice.

"Unmerited favor," a definition of God's grace, was simply not in my vocabulary. Total acceptance and unconditional love were only terminology to me. I struggled to apply those terms personally.

Eventually, my performance orientation took its toll. I simply could not keep up with the demand.

I then made a very unfortunate transition. No longer did I try to live up to the expectations of others. Having internalized this driving force, I began making these harsh requirements of myself.

I sought the counsel of a very wise person who helped me understand how I had gotten myself into such a dilemma and how to unravel the confusion.

I began to search the Scriptures carefully and purposefully. The apostle Paul made it clear in Ephesians 2:8 that it is "by grace" that we have been saved. He spent most of his time in the Book of Galatians explaining that just as we are saved by God's grace, we are also perfected (brought to maturity) by His grace.

As I focused my mind on this, I began to comprehend that grace means God accepts me just as I am. He does not require or insist that I measure up to someone else's standard of performance. He loves me completely, thoroughly, and perfectly. There's nothing I can do to add to or detract from that love. He forgives me. Nothing I have ever done or will ever do is beyond the reach of His mercy and grace to forgive.

Even as I began to understand His grace, my mind still needed deprogramming. Its "software" had received inaccurate data. During the formative years of my life, I assumed God's demands were similar to but greater than those of my colleagues, friends, and family. I tried hard to please people and even harder to please Him. Yet, my self-effort, though well-intentioned, was thwarting my spiritual growth.

I needed first to understand and experience His grace. Once I grasped that, I could pursue and enjoy healthy relationships that reflected God's love. I stopped needing to perform.

Isn't it interesting that we are products of our early years? If someone is consistently lied to as a child, he will have difficulty trusting as an adult. If one is molested in childhood, she will not easily experience intimacy as an adult. If abandoned as a child, it is very hard to experience security in adult relationships.

Unwilling to let His children stay trapped in those liabilities, the Lord often engineers circumstances to reveal deep needs and provides people and insight to cause healing and growth. This is what He did for me. I performed as a child in order to be accepted. As an adult I did the same. Even in my relationship with the Lord, I assumed I would win His approval by my achievements—even though, intellectually, I knew better.

Eventually, as I was able to define my problem, determine my own misconceptions, realize why I had them and ultimately put my faith in the trustworthiness of a loving God, I began to grow and change. I actually felt it in my person, in my soul.

With those changes came an ability to experience not only His love and acceptance, but also a freedom that I had never known before. Paul said, "It was for freedom that Christ set us free" (Galatians 5:1). What a verse! Christ did not set us free from one thing so we could be enslaved by another. He set us free so we could enjoy freedom in Him.

God not only used my experience to show me that performance does not work, He gave me His Word to help me overcome my human tendencies. He surrounded me with a body of caring, supportive believers who genuinely loved me for who I am, not for what I can do. They were consistent, faithful, and devoted to me.

At last, I am on my way to freedom: Freedom from the demands and expectations of others; freedom from my fear of failure; freedom from the need to perform; freedom from concern about my own acceptance. I'm learning to experience God's grace, to accept others where they are and let them be who God wants them to be. I'm discovering that I am not responsible for running the world. And best of all, I'm finding the freedom to enjoy freedom.

I learned many wonderful things from my family, and I am indebted to them for all they taught me. But it was God who helped me realize that His grace, His acceptance, is what gives my life meaning. He has been my greatest teacher and has taught me my greatest lesson: He loves me just as I am.

Ruth Bell Graham

WORRY AND WORSHIP CANNOT LIVE IN THE SAME HEART

Ruth Bell Graham and her evangelist husband, Billy, have made their mark for the glory of God upon the entire world.

Born in China to Dr. and Mrs. L. Nelson Bell, medical missionaries at the Presbyterian Hospital three hundred miles north of Shanghai, Ruth met Billy while a student at Wheaton College. In 1943, after graduating from Wheaton, they were married.

Ruth became a pastor's wife for a brief period in Western Springs, Illinois. When Dr. Graham became a full-time evangelist, the Grahams made their home in Montreat, North Carolina. They have five children, nineteen grand-children, and numerous great-grandchildren.

Ruth is the author of several books and an avid reader.

Because she has so much to share, she is in great demand as a speaker. But she mostly defers to her husband, saying, "One speaker in the family is enough."

The Bible says the older women should teach younger women.[1] Though Ruth is not that much older than I, she is one of the women I have most admired, observed, and loved. Never have I known a wiser, more Christlike woman ready to share her husband and herself with the world. She is a modern Proverbs 31 woman, a model for me and millions of others.

This account of her personal dependence upon God in the "storms" of life is typical of how she copes with daily encounters.

The rumble of thunder was only a distant threat. But the wind in the firs beside the stream, and the oaks and pines between the bedroom window and the street, announced the storm was on its way.

All my life I have loved storms. But then, I have only experienced them from the shelter of a solidly built house, and as a child, with the warm conviction that with Mother and Daddy near, nothing really bad could happen.

The wind rose menacingly, and there was a sudden crack of thunder directly overhead. Soon I heard the patter of little feet and sensed a small presence in the room. I heard a whispered "Mother?" That was all.

The covers were thrown back in comforting welcome as one or more small, night-clad forms would slip in (depending on the severity of the storm). There, lovingly encircled, we snuggled safely together under the covers, listening to the storm, unafraid. As nature once more grew quiet, we drifted off to sleep.

In later years, when I knew they were all enduring their own individual storms, I would lie awake wishing I could share them.

At night, it was as if I could hear a whispered "Mother?" Only there was no one there. I sensed the distant thunder, and all I could do was pray.

Then came the time when the Lord taught me to utilize more fully these times of prayer in the early hours of the day.

It was early in the morning in another country. Exhausted as I was, I awoke around three o'clock. The name of someone I loved dearly flashed into my mind. It was like an electric shock. Instantly I was wide awake. I knew there would be no more sleep for me the rest of the night. So I lay there and prayed for the one who was trying hard to run away from God. When it is dark and the imagination runs wild, there are fears that only a mother can understand.

Suddenly the Lord said to me, "Quit studying the problems and start studying the promises." Now God has never spoken to me audibly, but there is no mistaking when He speaks.

So I turned on the light, got out my Bible, and the first verse that came to me was Philippians 4:6: "Be careful for nothing; but in every thing by prayer and supplication *with thanksgiving* let your requests be made known unto God." And verse 7: "And the peace of God, which passeth all understanding, shall keep your hearts and minds through Christ Jesus." Or, as the *Amplified Version* has it, "Do not fret or have any anxiety about anything, but in every cir-

cumstance and in everything by prayer and petition [defi-
nite requests] *with thanksgiving* continue to make your
wants known to God" (emphasis added).

Suddenly I realized that the missing ingredient in my
prayers had been "with thanksgiving." So I put down my
Bible and spent time worshiping God for who He is and
what He is. This covers more territory than any one mortal
can comprehend. Even contemplating what little we do
know dissolves doubts, reinforces faith, and restores joy. I
began to thank God for giving me this one I loved so dearly
in the first place. I even thanked Him for the difficult spots
that taught me so much.

And do you know what happened? It was as if someone
suddenly turned on the lights in my mind and heart, and
the little fears and worries which, like mice and cockroaches,
had been nibbling away in the darkness, suddenly scuttled
for cover.

That was when I learned that worship and worry cannot
live in the same heart: they are mutually exclusive.[2]

Pattie Harris

OVERCOMING DEPRESSION

Before joining the staff of Campus Crusade for Christ, Pattie Harris spent many years in the educational field. She served as an elementary music instructor, an early childhood education specialist, and an educational administrator in the United States and Africa.

As a Campus Crusade staff member with Christian Leadership Ministries, she ministers to college professors and administrators in Delaware and Southeastern Pennsylvania. Her campus ministry has included short-term projects in Kenya and South Africa. She is presently working toward a graduate degree in theology at Biblical Theological Seminary in order to integrate teaching of religion courses into her college campus ministry.

She continues to conduct workshops concerning many areas of the Christian life around the country and in the Carribbean.

Here Pattie shares her secret for overcoming depression and living joyfully and victoriously despite difficult circumstances in her life.

For most of my life I have battled a pervasive sense of sadness that I can only describe as a type of low-grade fever.

Knowing that I have a melancholy personality, for years I thought my despondency was normal. I believed that just as the universe needs to have both positive and negative forces to be in balance, so my personality was created to balance the optimists of the world. Once a friend asked me to imagine a scene of a young girl walking in the woods. True to character, I saw a dark and foreboding forest with danger lurking all around.

What I still find hard to understand is that I received some satisfaction in my feelings of dejection.

While it was true that my spirit was constantly downcast, my circumstances belied my negative outlook. I came from a loving family. Having only one child, my parents worked and sacrificed to provide every educational and cultural advantage for me. Because I had experienced so many positive times in my life, on the surface I would come across as a pleasant, cheerful person. Throughout this time, I managed to carry on a career as a teacher and educational administrator and as a staff member of a Christian organization, ministering to the spiritual needs of career and professional women. Ironically, I was trying to be a role model of the joyful Christian life.

By my thirties, the sadness had developed into a ghastly

sense of dread. In my forties, the feelings of dejection were full-blown depressions. Since I grew up believing that discussing your feelings was in bad taste, only a few people knew about my secret malady. I called upon my personal cheering squad night and day, and they faithfully listened to my moaning and groaning. Through their encouragement and prayers I would receive temporary emotional relief.

It took years for me to articulate why I was grieving. My thoughts had become stuck on the chapter of my life called "Disappointments and Unfulfilled Dreams." Here I was, approaching age fifty, still single and still suffering from an affliction of many single women—hope deferred. Time was moving on and leaving me behind to mourn myself into poor health.

The turning point came at my lowest moment. For several days, I had not been able to concentrate. Every time I looked at my work on the computer screen that I had been trying to write for weeks, I felt nauseated. Lately, my hours at work had been spent in an endless cycle of staring at the computer hoping for one clear idea, pacing my office floor, making inaudible screams, and heading back to the computer again.

Finally one day I said, "This is ridiculous," and went for professional help. I asked a counselor who was leasing an office in our suite, "What does it feel like to have a nervous breakdown?"

"One symptom," she said, "is the feeling of losing control."

I sighed. "That's what I'm feeling right now. What should I do?"

"Pattie, if you're really feeling that way, I think the best thing for you to do is to check yourself into a hospital."

I didn't expect that response. I wanted to hear something soothing and comforting. But hospitalization! I was both horrified and indignant. The whole world would now know that I was having a nervous breakdown. It's one thing to *feel* pitiful, but it's another for everybody else to regard you as pitiful.

I DETERMINED TO SEEK JOY, CLAIM IT, SEIZE IT, TREASURE IT, AND DELIGHT IN IT.

The next morning, as usual, I struggled to lift my head from the pillow. But this time I was enraged about my miserable state. "I'm *not* going to any hospital! I can't afford it. Plus, a lot of people are depending on me, so there's no time to be away."

My anger became the energy I needed to scream out to God in complete abandonment, "God, I need help, and I refuse to go to anyone but You! You will be my psychiatrist, my psychologist. I will seek Your face and claim Your promises."

God did meet my needs in a dramatic way. I never found it necessary to seek professional help again, though I don't criticize those who do.

I began to think about a verse that someone had shared with me many years ago about King David.

> David was greatly distressed, for the people spoke of stoning him, because the soul of all the people was grieved, every man for his sons and his daughters. But David strengthened [encouraged] himself in the Lord his God (1 Samuel 30:6).

David was in a no-win situation. For years he had cunningly escaped death at the hands of Saul and his army.

Now his own men blamed him for the kidnapping of their wives and children by a band of raiders and were planning to execute him. Who was there for David? No wife, no friends, no support group, no comforting book to read. No doubt David felt depressed.

Whatever happened between David and God resulted in renewed courage, confidence, and ultimately a victorious rescue operation. I asked God to show me how to encourage myself in Him as David had done. That day I began one of the greatest adventures in my Christian life.

Now, when the dark clouds begin to descend over my head and I start to focus on my hurts and disappointments, I put my self-encouragement formula into practice.

First, *be joyful.* I reason that if it is true that:

- in God's presence there is fullness of joy (Psalm 16:11)
- Jesus wants me to have His joy (John 15:11)
- it was joy that kept Christ on the cross (Hebrews 12:2)
- the joy of the Lord is my strength (Nehemiah 8:10)

then I must *always* have this joy. As an act of the will, I chose to be joyful. I determined to seek it, claim it, seize it, treasure it, and delight in it.

Second, *meditate on specific promises of God as they relate to my need.* In doing this I keep in mind what God has to say:

- about Himself
- about me
- about His love for me

As I read and meditate on the psalms, David's record of his times with the Lord, and affirm the truths recorded in them, explosions of joy take place in my heart. I actually feel the adrenalin surging in my body. I can bound out of bed and face my daily problems head on. Living by the spiritual principles I have observed in the life of David has taught me the greatest lesson of my life.

My life is radically different as a result. I tell people that I am happier and more content than I have ever been. I recognize that I may sound as though I am ignoring the hard times. So I follow up with, "I still have the same problems, the dark clouds descend, the pain remains, but now I know what to do about them. I have learned how to encourage myself in the Lord."

Jeanne Hendricks

"'Tis Death That Makes Life Live"

A native of Philadelphia, Pennsylvania, Jeanne grew up in a solid Christian home. Local church and youth activities were a vital part of her life. She attended Houghton College in New York and Wheaton College in Illinois and received her B.A. degree in journalism from Southern Methodist University in Dallas. She also has formal training in business and the Bible and has studied the American family and aging in America at Harvard University.

She has taken several study/ministry trips to Europe, Africa, the Middle East, and the Orient.

Married to Howard G. Hendricks, distinguished professor and chairman of the Center for Christian Leadership of Dallas Theological Seminary, she is the mother of four married children and has several grandchildren.

Professionally, Jeanne has been a pastor's wife and teacher, as well as a medical secretary and freelance writer. Presently *she is in great demand as a speaker for women's conferences and youth seminars, and she teams with her husband in teaching family life conferences.*

You will be inspired as Jeanne shares the lessons she learned while conquering her fear of death and discovering her real purpose in life.

Viewed from the heights of grandmotherhood, life tends to hide its shadows. When eyewitnesses are gone, older women tend to "forget" failures. And little-girl fantasies, wrinkled with age, can come alive to retouch family histories.

I am tempted to downplay my early tussle with the concept of death because for so long it held me by the throat. But I crave an ability to recall the way it really was because only then can I tell you what I learned about living and how I learned it from what Job called "the king of terrors."

For years I didn't even know I needed to learn a lesson about people. Like every newborn baby, I arrived into the world and people were there, talking and being who they were. I imitated them and didn't ask questions. But when suddenly some were not there any longer, that got my attention.

Robert Browning's words describe my experience:

You never know what life means till you die. Even throughout life, 'tis death that makes life live.

Death has made its statement in our world. It is the irreversible closure, the period—or exclamation point—or question mark, at the end of the human sentence. It is the most profound lights out, the end of the road, the final crush, the last ultimate humiliation of humanity. And it struck paralyzing fear into my six-year-old being when I met it head-on for the first time.

Aunt Carrie lived close by; she was my frequent baby-sitter, the mother of four favorite cousins, and it was at her home in suburban Philadelphia where our family ate nearly every Sunday dinner. Then came a stormy spring night when I sat on my daddy's lap in her darkened living room and saw her corpse.

Nobody could explain why to my satisfaction. My cousins seemed as confused as I was, and the adults in the family just didn't say much. At home Dad told me that she had too much fat around her heart; nevertheless, Aunt Carrie was gone and nothing was the same.

A decade passed, years in which uncertainty about life and death grew for me. During that time, I made a personal commitment of my life to Jesus Christ. I understood, at least in theory, the ultimate answer to death, but the churning torment of loss when a loved one was irretrievably gone had not been alleviated. I had no label for my inward terror, much less did I understand my real need. In no way was I prepared for another shattering loss.

This time I was alerted, but I plugged my ears. A childless couple who had become family friends when I was about eight years old began to invite me to spend time with them. Uncle Floyd and Aunt Grace enchanted me as they took me with them in their shiny car to visit their wonderful German relatives. One of his uncles owned a candy shop; another one had a small farm. All of them were marvelous storytellers and happy, friendly, and kind. My difficult early teen years were highlighted with these loving and high-spirited people who introduced me to having good clean fun. Then without warning, Uncle Floyd pulled me aside during a weekend retreat and told me he loved me and wanted to say goodbye; he was having heart surgery on his "leaky pump."

"No!" I protested. "You'll get better; I know you will!"

But he knew intuitively, and about a week later, the dreaded call came from Aunt Grace. I wanted to run away and scream, to somehow undo the personal knot that was choking me, to change it all. Instead I had to stand beside the casket and face the truth, but I could not bear to look at Uncle Floyd's face. I closed my eyes and tried to deny; I simply had no coping mechanism.

Every year we celebrated Christ's resurrection. I had memorized parts of 1 Corinthians 15. I had sung often, "O death, where is thy sting? O grave, where is thy victory?" But the monster kept pursuing me and moving in ever closer. As a young adult I tried to become a bit more philosophical. When three of my own babies died before they were born, I pretended that it hadn't really happened. But there was no escape; the day came when Mother told me that Dad was terminally ill with cancer.

No, not my daddy! He's too big and strong and warm and loving—God will make an exception. I believed it and I went home and sat with Mother in the living room and pleaded in prayer for Dad's miraculous recovery. But the disease persisted and took its deadly toll. Dad's ready wit and engaging personality faded. He whispered hoarsely and scanned me with serious and piercing eyes. I knew him well because we had often talked together, and he had many times given me advice that was filled with uncanny insight and common sense. Now it was his last opportunity, and

God allowed him to share with me the most important counsel he had ever given to this second daughter with whom a mutual trust had grown over the years. Dad held out his wasted arm to me and began to fill in my blanks.

"Honey, don't be sad. God gave me many years and that's what counts. Now, He's letting you and Howie and your youngsters carry on. So, you just use your life for the Lord. Just do what He tells you. And I'll be seeing you again..."

With months to prepare, I was still not ready for the icy words, "He's gone." Never had I wept with tears so bitter, so unable to be turned off. Never was there a colder, more bleak October day than that dreadful afternoon when Dad, my source of comfort and consolation since birth, sank into the sod.

Aunt Carrie had left a mysterious emptiness. Uncle Floyd had said he loved me, but I resented his absence. Dad had tried to prepare me, and finally I was beginning to understand. Death *is* bigger and stronger than I am, but I don't have to be its victim. I can learn from it.

Falling asleep has always been one of my best accomplishments. But after Dad died, I found myself lying awake in bed with a deep sense of loss and sadness. I often woke up in the middle of the night and cried bitter tears because he was no longer available to me—or was he? I began to think back over the words he had spoken.

First, there was the hope—"I'll see you again..." Of course, that is exactly what Jesus told His disciples when He was going to the cross. Death was not the end, not the real end.

Second, Dad was gone, but I was still here with my family. He had said that it was now my turn—he handed me the torch.

A new resolve began to set into my thinking. The little oft-repeated couplet surfaced: "Only one life, 'twill soon be past. Only what's done for Christ will last." Gradually I began to gain strength from remembering that parting scene by the bedside. Like a transfusion of spiritual vitamins, my goals crystallized. I began to see what Paul meant by the defanging of death and the grave.

Death is neutralized by life when that life continues in another warrior who "fights the good fight." The grave is a mere formality in the total scheme of God's grace.

When Mother died in my home, after twenty-three years of widowhood, I was sad, but also full of a deep joy that I had been privileged to come into the world as the product of her—and Dad's—love. The emptiness and void were there, but they were overshadowed by a sense of challenge: It's my turn now.

Jesus speaks to me with full force: "He who loves his life will lose it...Unless a grain of wheat falls into the ground and dies, it remains alone; but if it dies, it produces much grain" (John 12:24,25). And so with full speed ahead, I aim to pour myself into other lives so that Christ may say of me, "Well done, good and faithful servant."

Aunt Carrie's death left me with a fear, based on ignorance, of people. I simply did not know how important they were and I took them for granted. Uncle Floyd's passing left me with a fear based on unwillingness to allow people to come in (and go out) of my life. Dad helped me look my fear in the face, to break it and melt it by using death as a harsh, but very effective, teacher.

Aunt Carrie had cared for me; Uncle Floyd had reached out to a quiet little girl and shared with her the mainstream of his life. Dad dispelled for me the seeming impossibility of facing death's horror.

Possibly the most amazing fallout from these three significant deaths was the implant of love for people. I was known as a shy child, a painfully insecure, timid, and self-conscious teen. Always concerned with what people would think of me, constantly avoiding public visibility, I was slow to realize that my purpose in life was simply to relate to other people. Like the payload on a three-stage rocket, I found myself catapulted into a life of serving people, touching them with the love and confidence I received from Christ. Best of all, funerals were no longer the numbing horrors of my early years.

Whether human beings divert attention from funerals with political parades or try to drown them with laughter and liquor, we all cower in the presence of death. It is impossible not to. Jesus Christ sweat drops of blood and suffered incredible agony in contemplation of His death; He took it seriously and so should we. No one escapes its clutches, but we can escape its consequences. Salvation through Christ means victory over the grave. His words to John are my ultimate consolation:

> Do not be afraid. I am the First and the Last. I am the Living One; I was dead, and behold I am alive for ever and ever! And I hold the keys of death and Hades (Revelation 1:17,18).

Kay Coles James

I, TOO, HAVE
A DREAM

Kay Coles James has been active in the development, implementation, and analysis of American public policy for the past twenty years in senior positions in the public and private sectors. Among other positions, she has been dean of the School of Government at Regent University, senior vice-president of the Family Research Council, associate director for the White House Office of National Drug Control Policy, and assistant secretary for public affairs at the U.S. Department of Health and Human Services.

A native of Virginia, she received her B.S. degree from Hampton Institute. Long interested in family issues, she is one of the founders and a former president of Black Americans for Life. In addition, she and her husband, Charles E. James, founded the National Family Institute in 1985 to address the crisis within the American family.

Having had experience in varied businesses as a supervi-

sor, personnel manager, and administrator, she gained recognition as a volunteer for social causes including equal housing opportunities in Virginia. She also served as a member of the board of the Family and Children's Services and the Richmond, Virginia, Metropolitan Crisis Pregnancy Center. In 1988 she was appointed a member of the White House Commission on Children and the White House Task Force on the Black Family.

She also has been the director of public affairs of the National Right to Life Committee in Washington, D.C. Her experiences with legislative efforts have made her comfortable with the media, conducting national press conferences and numerous presentations before audiences in the U.S., England, and Ireland.

Mrs. James and her husband have three children and reside in Chesapeake, Virginia.

She balances beautifully a professional career and her strong commitment to biblical principles. In the following story she relates how the Christlike love of a young white girl and two white women touched her life and kept her from becoming a bitter, resentful, and angry woman over the racial injustices she has suffered since childhood.

As a woman I am constantly juggling many balls—some crystal, some rubber.

One of my crystal balls—our son, Robert—asked me to come to his elementary school and give a talk for Black History Month. The commitment was easy to make when it was weeks away, but by the time the day arrived the calendar was tight and I was called upon to do one of my best juggling acts.

I'll confess, I didn't view this as one of my more important speeches, and my preparation was minimal—just a few notes scribbled on a piece of paper. It could easily have been confused with one of Robert's homework assignments. When the children started filing in and I really began to focus on the importance of Black History Month, I suddenly became aware of the significance of this event and the tremendous opportunity to touch those young lives. I silently prayed and asked God's forgiveness for not having spent more time in preparation, and for not recognizing this as a truly crystal-ball opportunity. I asked for His help and guidance.

My assigned task was to share with the students what it was like growing up as a black child in the South during the Civil Rights struggle. I wanted to paint word pictures for the children so they could not only appreciate the facts, but perhaps even see themselves living my experience.

This is the story I told them:

I want to tell you a true story. I know the story is true because it happened to me. There are two other main characters, and when I finish, I want you to tell me which one you want to be like.

When I was in the sixth grade like some of you, my parents told me that the time had come to integrate the schools. Integrate means to mix. In those days, black children and white children could not go to school together. There were many white people who thought that because I was black, I should go to a separate school, that I should only live in certain neighborhoods, have certain jobs, and go to certain churches. Why? I still don't completely understand. I suppose they were afraid of my family and me because we were different. We are African Americans. Our skin is darker, our cultural experience is different. Often people fear what they don't know and understand.

The first day of junior high school can be a frightening experience under the best of circumstances. But for me it was a nightmare. When I arrived, there were police cars, reporters, and angry parents. Some held on to their children and refused to let them come into the school; others walked cautiously past the crowd and entered the building. I was so confused. Why were those people saying those mean things to me? Why were they so angry with me? What had I done?

My parents walked me to the principal's office and told him that I was being left in his care in excellent condition and when they picked me up at three o'clock, they expected to find me in the same condition. I think he got the message. But the day did not get any better. The name-calling was bad, but constantly being stuck with pins as we changed classes was horrible. And although being stuck with pins hurt, being spat upon hurt even more.

Some of the teachers did their part to make us feel unwelcome. When my homeroom teacher read the menu for the next day, she said: "Tomorrow we will have vegetable soup, grilled cheese sandwiches, fruit cups, and brownies. Lord only knows why they're serving brownies, we have enough of *them* here already!"

The class laughed. I cried.

The harassment continued. The students kept up their pranks and the teachers tried to discourage the black kids by giving us bad grades no matter how good our work was. I wanted to give up and go back to my all-black school where the teachers cared about me and I had been president of the student government. Life was just fine in my segregated school.

Several months into the school year, things were not going any better. One day, as I was walking to class, a big white guy came up behind me and pushed me down the steps. As I tumbled down the stairs, I twisted my back and ended up in a heap at the foot of the steps. That was obviously not enough for him, so he kicked my books and scattered them in the corridor.

A crowd gathered. Some laughed, others cheered. Willard gloated as he continued kicking my books. A white girl stepped from the crowd and gathered up my books, then helped me stand as best I could. As she led me away toward the principal's office, the crowd turned on Ann.

"Nigger lover! Nigger lover!"

I was out of school for several weeks with a back injury, and when I returned I looked for Ann. I wanted to know if she had faced any trouble for trying to help me. She said that some kids were mean to her but they weren't nice kids anyway, so she really hadn't lost any friends. A friendship developed between Ann and I.

As I told my story, I explained to the children that even though it was more than twenty-five years ago, I still remembered Willard and Ann. Willard stands as a symbol of all the ugly, hateful experiences I had. Ann helped to shape the person I am today. I was well on my way to being a bitter, resentful, angry woman. She touched my life and helped shape my character for the better.

I then challenged my listeners to become "Anns" and

not "Willards."

I encouraged them to ask me questions. That's when I received my Black History Month blessing. A cute little white child raised his hand and asked, "Mrs. James, what's a nigger?" A few kids snickered, and he looked hurt. I asked him his age and he said he was ten. I wanted to hug him, his parents, and his teachers. They were obviously doing something right.

Unfortunately, the racism I experienced was not confined to junior high school. As I grew up I suffered institutional as well as individual racism. And while I am encouraged today by a young white child in Fairfax County, I know that racism is still a force to be reckoned with in our schools, in the work place, our communities, and our churches. Why, then, do I not live my life in anger and bitterness? It is because over the years the Lord continued to place "Anns" in my life, and I finally accepted as reality the biblical principles of forgiveness and the transcendent nature of God's love. And I always remember that faith itself is a mystery that demands trust.

IN THEM I FOUND THE UTTERLY SELF-EMPTYING KIND OF CHRISTLIKE LOVE.

While in college, I met two women through InterVarsity Christian Fellowship. Joyce and Beth, both white, richly amplified the friendship I had experienced in junior high. In them I also found the utterly self-emptying kind of Christlike love. It was a love devoted not only to the content of my character, but to its Christian maturation as well.

They each had an emphasis in their witness to Christianity. Joyce represented the power of grace, Beth the presence of obedience to God's law. I was confident of the un-conditional love that I received from both of them. Their effect on me is incalculable. It came as no surprise to any-one who knew me well that when my daughter was born she was named Elizabeth Joyce James.

As a part of my private Black History Month celebration, I reread Dr. Martin Luther King Jr.'s famous "I Have a Dream" speech. One of my favorite quotes became even more real to me:

> I have a dream my four little children will one day live in a nation where they will not be judged by the color of their skin but by the content of their character. I have a dream today!

What would my character be had Ann, Joyce, and Beth not entered my life? It frightens me to think of what I may have become. It is God's miracle that the Christian love of one white girl and two white women made Dr. King's words so important in my life.

In the mystery of God's wisdom, Dr. King's dream came true for me in the redemptive work of the Holy Spirit.

I, too, have a dream.

Margaret Jensen

THE LESSON OF THE HIGH BUTTON SHOES

When most people reach their late sixties they contemplate retirement. When Margaret Jensen reached her late sixties, she was just getting started in a personal ministry that has endeared her to hundreds of thousands of readers.

It began in 1983 with the release of First We Have Coffee, *Margaret's collection of warm-hearted personal stories centered around her godly Norwegian mother. The book generated so much interest that a major book club offered it as a main selection—and the rest, as they say, is history.* First We Have Coffee *became a national best-seller.*

In the years since, appreciative audiences across the United States and Canada have dubbed Margaret Jensen "America's favorite Christian storyteller." Margaret keeps a travel and speaking calendar that would exhaust a healthy twenty-one-year-old, and by popular demand she has authored several additional books.

The following story of high button shoes tells how Margaret learned a lesson that has had an impact on her life since childhood. Today, it is one of the most requested stories in her repertoire.

I had just exchanged a gift certificate for a pair of expensive shoes from an exclusive shoe store. I proudly clutched the gold-braided handle of the fancy box that held the navy blue pumps. Never had I owned such beautiful shoes—a perfect match for my navy blue suit! With hurried steps I headed toward the parking lot to turn my car homeward.

When I rounded the corner I found myself in front of a small shoe repair shop. I stopped! My gold-braided box fell limply to my side. In the window stood a pair of old-fashioned high button shoes. Hot tears clouded my vision. In a moment I was a ten-year-old child again, back in my home in Canada…

I needed shoes! I *always* needed shoes! Papa traveled throughout the province of Saskatchewan to minister to the needs of the Scandinavian immigrants, so our bank account was Philippians 4:19: "My God shall supply all your needs." He did—but not always my way!

The arrival of the "missionary barrel" was an annual event in our home. Every outdated relic from the past seemed to find its way into that barrel: moth-eaten coats, hats with plumes and feathers, corsets with the stays, threadbare silks and satins, shoes of all sizes and shapes.

Mama used the hand-me-downs from the missionary barrel to make clothes for her children. She wasted nothing. Buttons, silks, and furs were transformed into beautiful dresses and coats. The scraps were put together for pallets for the floor, or sewn into quilts. We never lacked quilts!

"Margaret," Papa called, "we have shoes!"

I started to run away. I had lived through enough missionary barrel debuts to know I probably wouldn't like the shoes Papa had found.

"I'm sure they won't fit," I replied as I kept running.

"Margaret!"

I stopped. I went to Papa and stared in horror when he held up the monstrosities: two pairs of high button shoes, a black pair and a brown pair. Oxfords were "in"; button shoes were "out"!

"Try them on." Papa left no room for discussion.

I complained that they were too big.

"*Ja*, that is good. We'll put cotton in the toes. They'll last a long time." No one argued with Papa.

Mama sensed my distress and tenderly said, "Margaret, we prayed for shoes, and now we have shoes. Wear your shoes with a thankful and humble heart. It is not so important what you have on the feet, but it is very important where the feet go. This could be one of life's valuable lessons." (No ten-year-old is interested in "valuable lessons.")

"OH GOD,

KEEP YOUR

MOUNTAINS, BUT

MOVE MY SHOES.

THANK YOU."

I knew better than to argue with God and Mama on this point, but I had a plan. Papa's sermons on faith told of Moses and the crossing of the Red Sea, and Daniel in the den of lions. "If you have faith, you can move mountains,"

Papa's voice echoed in my mind. I knew what to do.

I carefully placed the shoes (buttonhook included!) beside my bedroom door and prayed, "Oh God, keep Your mountains, but move my shoes. Thank You."

The next morning I fully expected the shoes to be gone. Was I in for a surprise. They were still there. Something went wrong! I had a strange suspicion that it might be related to Mama's "valuable lessons."

"Hurry, Margaret," Mama called. "It's time for Sunday school."

I buckled up my galoshes over those awful high button shoes and reluctantly trekked off in the snow to Sunday school. *If I can keep my galoshes on, no one will see my horrible shoes,* I thought to myself. *Tomorrow I'll think of something else.*

Upon arriving at church, I carefully wiped off my galoshes and started into class. A booming voice called out, "Margaret, no one goes into Sunday school class with galoshes on. You're dripping."

Slowly I unbuckled my galoshes, and there I stood, for all the world to see, in my embarrassing old high button shoes. My face grew hot as I felt my classmates' silent pity.

Then my friend Dorothy came in, and she was also carefully wiping off her galoshes. The same voice of authority boomed out, "Dorothy, take off your galoshes. You're dripping."

Slowly, Dorothy removed her galoshes...and stood before us in a pair of hand-knit socks. She had no shoes. There we were, two ten-year-old girls, learning life's "valuable lesson."

"Good morning, young ladies," came the crisp English accent of our beloved Sunday school teacher. Mr. Avery, a frail, elderly, blue-eyed gentleman with white hair and a goatee, quietly assessed the situation.

Each Sunday, as we formed a large circle in our class, Mr. Avery chose two children to sit beside him. It was almost like sitting next to God. This morning Mr. Avery announced, "Dorothy, you sit here on one side of me and Margaret, you sit here on the other."

The shoes and socks were forgotten. He had picked us! Mr. Avery had picked us! My old shoes and Dorothy's socks didn't matter to Mr. Avery. He had picked us anyway! I remember very little of what he said that morning—but I'll never forget what he did.

When it was time to leave, Dorothy and I pulled on our galoshes and walked out into the snow. Our heads were held high—Mr. Avery had picked us!

Mama was right. It is not so important what is on our feet, but where our feet go.

Alice McIntire

A WILLINGNESS TO BE USED

Alice McIntire loved entertaining as a monologist, but her life's passion was teaching the Bible. Throughout her life she taught different groups from youth and college age to the socialites of the San Diego area.

She and her husband, Eugene, a druggist, were active in San Diego area churches, including La Jolla Presbyterian Church and San Diego Presbyterian Church. They also helped to found a church in Rancho Santa Fe, an exclusive area of San Diego.

Although Alice went to be with the Lord in November 1998 at the age of 94, her impact on my life continues.

I met Alice when Bill and I traveled from Hollywood to La Jolla, California, with a group of students for ministry work. Although Alice is probably twenty years older than I, it was one of those relationships where we were mutually crazy about one another from the moment we met. She took great interest in me as a young bride in ministry. She encouraged me and prayed for me consistently. We talked on the phone regularly and became wonderful friends. She loved God in front of me, and we talked about Christ often. As I watched her walk with God, I thought, I can do that. *Alice had a remarkable impact on my life because she believed in me, and believed in what God could do in and through me.*

The following story reveals that, no matter what our circumstances, God uses us if we are willing.

Pink-clad angels frolicking on bookshelves and countertops matched the carpet, couches, and drapes of my Southern California home. The chatter of thirty to forty women and the clink of their tea cups quieted as I opened my Bible class in prayer.

Since childhood, I had dreamed of being, not a Bible teacher, but a monologist. Let me explain.

Being a monologist was exciting and challenging. You portrayed the actors in a story, not by describing them, but by taking their parts as they spoke to one another. Being a monologist was demanding. You assumed many different characters—parents, grandparents, children, aunts, uncles, and a whole list of eccentric people as they talked together and unfolded the plot. You conversed person-to-person by turning your head slightly to the left and to the right. As a monologist you were on stage without a single note or cue card to remind yourself of the next line.

Growing up in Los Angeles, I used to go to the theater to hear Ruth Draper and Helen Hayes, the chief monologists of their day. Their material ranged from serious drama to humor, all done from memory. The audience never missed having live actors on stage. The monologist's portrayal of the characters was so convincing that everyone sat in rapt attention throughout the program.

How could I get started in this exacting art? I found a book on monologues but the material was so outdated that it could be used for neither drama nor humor. The next best thing was to tackle writing it myself. This wasn't as hard as it sounded since I took excerpts from real life as I encountered them. In the beginning I practiced on school groups. They were usually friendly and most responsive.

The memory work, though extensive, was the least of my problems. The clear depiction of different conversations through voice changes was the most demanding aspect. As I continued to improve, I was rewarded with generous audience approval.

My agent, Gertrude Purple Gorham, arranged for all the Southern California Women's Clubs to meet together at the Ebell Theater in Los Angeles to hear a sample repertoire of several of her artist clients. As a result, I was booked for appearances by a number of clubs and had to have at least an hour's worth of memorized programs ready to go.

Soon I was also having wonderful opportunities before civic and church groups. One night, after a performance in Hollywood, I was offered a screen test at Fox Studios. I told them I appreciated the offer, but turned it down as I was content with what I was doing.

As it turned out, my life was about to change in other directions. My husband, Gene, was transferred to La Jolla, just north of San Diego. In order to continue my work in Los Angeles, I asked my agent to book my performances there three days in a row. I would stay over and then return home to San Diego, where requests were also coming in. Soon after that our son Mike came along. My new responsibilities curtailed my out-of-town trips and I took on more local appearances.

For special occasions such as Christmas and Easter, I turned to the Bible for inspirational material and discovered my audiences welcomed it. I began to see the need in people for spiritual help, so I introduced little bits of Scripture at first, then added more and more. I found that the drama plots from the Bible proved to be exciting material for the women's groups I addressed.

Finally I wove together many favorite passages from the Pauline epistles and memorized them. When I presented these as a personal letter to each listener from the apostle Paul, I was overwhelmed with the emotional response. Soon other groups were asking for a repeat performance. To my amazement, some 400 women gathered together to put on a surprise luncheon for me at which time they "demanded" that I make a recording of "A Letter from Paul." The explosive reaction to this record was like starving people grasping for food. Christian Education specialist Dr. Henrietta C. Mears said, "This is a record that can be heard over and over again with increasing interest because the Word of God lives. I wish that this record could make its way around the world, and that it might be in every home."

After learning about Dr. Mears' Bible classes in Los Angeles, I realized people were just as eager for something like that where I lived. So I held a tea in my home and asked the women three questions:

- Would they be willing to open their homes for a Bible class?

- Would they be willing to teach a Bible class?
- Would they be willing to attend a Bible class?

Some answered "Yes" to all three questions, and everyone wanted to be in a class. As a result, Bible classes sprang up around San Diego County where the women learned to memorize Scripture and to honor God in their lives.

I had accepted Christ as my Savior when I was eight years old and, over the years, taught the church Sunday school curriculum to various age groups. But it is one thing to teach in that setting and another thing to launch out with your own material in a Bible class of women from various backgrounds. It was a new adventure which prompted me to study the Bible as never before. Whereas many people go to seminary to learn how to teach the Bible, I had to study on my own night and day to keep ahead of my students. As women's lives were changed through the Living Word, God showed me this was all the applause I needed. My monologue programs faded in importance as I gradually gave them up. Movies and television have replaced this ancient art in today's society, but nothing can replace the Word of God.

The Bible classes kept in close touch with one another so when a special event was planned we could spread the message quickly. In 1964, two weeks before Billy Graham was scheduled to be in San Diego, we decided to organize a luncheon as part of the preparation for the crusade. We were told it couldn't be done in such a short time. The announcement went out to our network of classes, and the largest crowd they had ever accommodated came to the Crown Room of the Hotel Del Coronado to hear Eleanor Searle Whitney, New York philanthropist, speak of God's grace in her life.

One Christmas we put on a party at the old El Cortez Hotel. The police had to be called to handle the traffic jam as over a thousand women came from the Bible classes. We continued these holiday luncheons with well-known speakers like Dr. Lane Adams and Dr. John McArthur for several years. We found this was an excellent time to invite new friends to the classes. Those get-togethers with dynamic speakers were so successful that at least one church in San Diego began a similar program on a monthly basis that is still continuing.

After several years of public life with exciting results, my activities were suddenly curtailed due to a severe accident. Bruised and battered, I found myself bedridden in my own home. This drastic change was very hard to accept. My room was turned into a hospital unit, with around-the-clock nurses brought in to care for me. I thought that, because of my physical limitations, my work for the Lord was over. However, I soon began sharing God's vast mercy and love again—this time with the nursing staff who cared for me day and night. These nurses became real friends to me. As they opened their hearts, I listened to their struggles. But I was not only a sympathetic listener. It was just natural for me to apply biblical principles to their problems. To my delight, some of these women trusted the Lord Jesus for salvation and began to grow spiritually.

One day my long-time friend Mary Stuard said to me, "Alice, you thought your work for the Lord was finished, but it's no such thing. You are still teaching the Bible, but in a different setting."

The truth of her statement flashed through my mind with a sudden burst of happiness. *I was still being used by the Lord.* God showed me that regardless of our circumstances, He still uses us if we are willing to be used. My advice is this: Be sure you don't give up too soon. Somewhere, sometime, there may be someone who is hurting, who needs your help and encouragement with biblical words. If necessary, use your bed as a pulpit and share the needed Scripture that will heal the wounded.

After thirty years I am still teaching. The Lord sent Betty Tafflinger, a Bible teacher, to assist me. Rather than using a lecture style, we developed a conversational method of teaching, with Betty and me discussing a selected passage of Scripture. Each week a group of women come to my home to memorize verses and learn how to pray in public. In the past I was speaking in schools, churches, and beautiful clubs for women. Now I am teaching in my home and enjoying every minute of it.

The greatest lesson I have ever learned was that you don't need to stand in front of large audiences to be used. God can use you in whatever circumstances He has placed you —even if you have to use your bed as a pulpit.

Yes, the applause of the world is sweet, but brief. The promises of God are *joyous* and *everlasting!*

Editor's note: Although Alice died after this story was written, she was used by God until He took her home.

Eleanor Page

GOD ANSWERS
IN WAYS BEYOND
OUR IMAGINATION

Tangy, buoyant, and feminine, Eleanor Page emanates a zest for life wherever she speaks. The primary aim of her life involves helping to meet the needs of women who "have it all" and still find something lacking in their lives.

Eleanor has shared God's love around the world. She's delightful at luncheons, motivating at seminars, encouraging at retreats—everyone is refreshed with a visit from Eleanor Page.

In 1972 she arrived in Washington, D.C., as a staff member of Campus Crusade for Christ to work at the Christian Embassy. She began to teach, train, and challenge congressional and senatorial wives and secretaries to be God's maximum women. She taught Bible classes in the White House and to members of the State Department during the

Nixon, Ford, and Reagan administrations.

She turned down a promising singing career to marry George Penzold Page of Norfolk, Virginia. After their marriage, much of Eleanor's life revolved around politics and the military. During World War II, her husband fought on the Normandy beachhead. Tragedy struck years later when George died of cancer.

Eleanor's tenacious spirit held on, however. After asking the question, "I must have a purpose. What could it be?" she discovered how to have an overflowing life with more spice and added dimension than she ever dreamed possible.

She is a beautiful woman whose energy exceeds that of most women even half her eighty years. She has been described as having the strength of Golda Meir, the grace of Amy Vanderbilt, and the courage of the biblical Queen Esther. I deeply appreciate her friendship and ministry.

In reading her story, you will find her radiance exciting and her faith refreshing as she tells about the beginnings of her fruitful ministry and how God miraculously answered her prayers.

During my years of Christian service, I have learned to rely on a simple formula for receiving answers to prayer: pray, believe, and go to God's Word for direction. By following this pattern, I have discovered how God can use our willingness to serve Him in ways beyond our imagination.

One of my most meaningful times in ministry has been among government and military leaders in Washington, D.C. Let me share how this opportunity came about in answer to prayer.

As the widow of a military man and trained in disciple-
ship and evangelism by Campus Crusade for Christ, I was a
natural candidate for ministry in the center of our nation's
political and military life.

To say that I was frightened when I learned of the opportunity would put it mildly. I knew no one in Washington, had no place to stay, and didn't know how to get started.
But I wanted to win souls for Christ and so accepted the
challenge.

I have never thought small; by nature I always strive for
the best. Not knowing what my mission field would entail,
I asked God for the White House and everything else under
its wing. I was willing and daring enough to believe that a
miracle-working God could use me to minister among government wives and secretaries and congressional and military officials from the White House to the Pentagon.

In accepting this challenge I was faced with some immediate needs, one of which was God's direction in what I
would do when I arrived in Washington.

I began to apply my formula for seeking His answer.

I read God's Word systematically, always picking up today where I left off yesterday. I keep a notebook and sometimes write down my impressions. Later, I go back to see
how these ideas fit into my circumstances as I live day by
day.

In seeking God's leading about my Washington ministry,
I found myself in the second chapter of Paul's epistle to
Titus:

> As for you, speak up for the right living that goes
> along with true Christianity. Teach the older women to

be quiet and respectful in everything they do…These older women must train the younger women to live quietly, to love their husbands and their children, and to be sensible and clean minded, spending their time in their own homes, being kind and obedient to their husbands, so that the Christian faith can't be spoken against by those who know them (Titus 2:1,3–5).

I began to see God's direction. I was a woman, a widow. I wasn't a spring chicken, and with my experiences of the past, I was primed for this mission. It was my calling to reach women wherever I could find them—in this case, Washington, D.C.—and share God's love and forgiveness, teaching them to be disciples for Christ.

I knew my calling. Now the next need: How do I find my mission fields?

The Bible tells us to let our requests be known to God. In bringing answers, He often uses people. I was asked to speak at a women's luncheon one day, and after I finished my talk an elderly woman came up to me. During our conversation, I told her I was leaving the area for Washington, D.C.

"Oh, I have a daughter in the Washington area who would love to hear you teach!" she exclaimed excitedly, then asked, "Do you have a place to stay?"

"No," I replied. "I'm going there tomorrow to find a real estate agent. I'm hoping he'll find me a place in 'Old Town' Alexandria."

She beamed. "My daughter lives in Alexandria."

"Is she a real estate agent?" I asked.

"No. She's a senator's wife. Virginia Spong."

Oh, my! My contact! I thought.

Not long after I arrived in Washington, God provided me with a comfortable apartment. After I settled in, Virginia invited me to her prayer group which met weekly in her home.

Word spreads fast in Washington, and by the time I had my telephone installed, I received a call from a general's widow inviting me to church.

"I understand you can teach the Bible," she said. "Will you come to my home and teach some of the military wives?"

I was amazed at how fast my ministry was falling into place. But I felt impatient to have all my requests for ministry fulfilled. "What about the White House?" I asked the Lord.

The way He arranged this for me was exciting. I had met a congressman at a seminar in Florida before moving to Washington. He had invited me to call his wife when I arrived in Washington to let them know where I was living. By the time I got in touch with her, she had heard that I was teaching a group of Senate wives.

"If I invited a group of congressional wives to my home for a Bible study, would you come and teach them?" she asked.

Would I!

I began the studies by teaching them God's plan for a wife as recorded in Titus 2. They seemed fascinated that God had a plan for women that they could follow.

These Bible studies began to generate much interest among the wives of our political and military leaders. One day several women who worked at the White House visited my new friend, the congressman's wife, and asked about our meetings.

"Do you suppose Eleanor Page would consider teaching

at the White House?" one inquired.

The call from the White House came to me a few days later, and my joy knew no bounds. God had answered every one of my prayers. Before the month was out, invitations to speak to the women in the Departments of Commerce, Transportation, and Health and Welfare filled my schedule.

One day after speaking to women at the Pentagon, a woman invited me to teach military wives in her and her husband's quarters at Fort Myer. She gathered a group of women, prepared tea, and introduced me as a military widow. She told them that I would teach them "God's Blueprint for Women." That study continued until she and her husband were transferred to another base. Then the commanding general's wife of Fort Myer invited the group to their quarters. Soon the women in this study began to reach others in their own spheres of influence.

Then the wife of the Chairman of the Joint Chiefs of Staff approached me to teach a group of wives of the admirals and generals in their quarters. These Bible studies lasted until he retired.

Can we pray and receive answers? You bet!

Through these experiences, I've learned how God operates. He says, "If you abide in Me, and My words abide in you, ask whatever you wish, and it shall be done for you" (John 15:7).

Do I believe it? With all my heart.

Dede Robertson

NO ROOM
FOR SELF-PITY

The wife of "Pat" Robertson, founder and chief executive
officer of the Christian Broadcasting Network, Dede Robert-
son was appointed in 1982 by Secretary of State George
Schultz as the principal U.S. delegate to the Inter-American
Commission of Women. She represented the U.S. at all offi-
cial IACW meetings and traveled in that capacity to Central
and South America.

With a master's degree from Yale University School of
Nursing, she is on the board of trustees of Regent University
and serves as a board member and vice president of the
Tidewater Area Birthright Organization. She also has been
secretary and member of the board of directors for CBN
since its founding in 1960.

She has traveled extensively in Asia, the Middle East,
and Central and South America. Selected Christian Woman
of the Year for 1986, she is an author, gifted interior design-

er, and antique expert.

Despite the many credits and successes in her life, Dede has struggled with bouts of self-pity. In her story she shares how she was restored to a life of peace and joy and gives insights to help us achieve better self-esteem.

Once upon a time there was a young girl who was her "daddy's little girl." She dreamed of a great knight on a white charger who would sweep her off her feet and marry her in a grandiose fashion. Then they would live happily ever after.

This little girl met her great knight. He swept her off her feet and, not under the best of circumstances, they eloped. Did they live happily ever after? Not for awhile.

Their lives were stormy. Time was always a problem. Not enough togetherness to satisfy her dreams. Then he found Jesus Christ as his Savior and decided to live on "faith." She didn't understand. She didn't believe that you could know Jesus. She became harsh and critical. She was anything but understanding. How the fur did fly on occasion!

Then she, too, discovered the wonder of knowing Jesus. She and her "knight" began to pray together, read the Word together, listen to the Lord together. They struggled and began a ministry together. They shared the hard times, but the good times in their lives made those hard times dim by comparison.

They had three children and a fourth one was expected. She had to curtail some of her activities outside the home, and he began working twenty-hour days. She could do nothing right—at least it appeared that way to her. Self-pity set in. Her dream world was becoming a nightmare.

Once self-pity took over, everything seemed to center around it, feeding it, making it bigger. Reality became unreality. Everything was seen and interpreted according to self-pity. Pity parties became a must.

The reality: The great knight was extremely shorthanded on staff. He was doing eight-hour shifts in two places, plus the day-to-day business of running a ministry. Funding was short, so in addition to balancing the books he had to appease the creditors.

Meanwhile, his wife was in the hospital to have a baby, and two of the three children were sick with measles, one dangerously ill. He was trying to keep house, cook three meals a day, take care of the sick children—all this on top of the demands of his ministry. No baby-sitter could be found except for a few hours a day.

The way she viewed it: He was gone all the time. He even had to pick up the mail and read it on the way to the hospital. (She asked the Lord to let her have the baby in the car to punish him!) She had several leisurely hours to wait in the hospital before the baby was born. Where were the flowers and praise? Where were those tender moments to share as you gaze at the precious life God entrusted to you both?

Postpartum depression set in with a bang. When all the children were well, the mother and mother-in-law visits were over, and she was physically recovered, it was still there—the awful loneliness, aching, self-pity, depression!

That little girl was me, Dede Robertson; the great knight was Pat Robertson. And I wasn't a little girl anymore! I was in my middle thirties. I had duties and responsibilities, yet I couldn't seem to get anything done but the bare essentials. I felt rejected, worthless, unhappy. I couldn't enjoy my friends. I couldn't play with my children, and I was so consumed with myself that I was unaware of how my attitude was affecting them. I couldn't read or study the Bible. I found it hard to pray except for "Please, Lord, get me out of this mess."

I couldn't share this with my husband; he seemed too busy. I couldn't share it with a friend; I had none that close. When the invitation to visit my parents over the Fourth of July came, I grabbed it. I just wanted to get away, even if it meant packing up all the children, spending a night on the train, and putting them in an environment different from that to which they were accustomed.

As we left, my husband told me of a church I might enjoy. I'm not one to go up to strangers and introduce myself, but suddenly going to this church became the most important thing for me to do.

It was a lovely church; the service was Bible centered. I met the pastor and his wife at the door and introduced myself. They remembered Pat and asked where I was staying. It turned out that they lived just two blocks away from my parents. In fact, they lived in the same house in which one of my high school friends had lived in.

Perhaps sensing my need, they graciously opened their home to me for visits, prayer, Bible study, and fellowship. I was over there at every possible opportunity. I sensed the same great love, peace, and joy in their home that I had known as a new Christian—that I had lost when I let self-pity take over my life.

Slowly, with their love and counsel, that peace, love, and

joy became a part of me once more. I can remember one prayer meeting where I just put my head back and began drinking in the Holy Spirit who was all around me. The Word of God came alive again, and oh! how I hungered for more of it.

Along with drinking in that love, peace, and joy, I became aware of how much God loved me. I knew He was responsible for all of this. I realized that He really cared about me. He was meeting my needs. He did not want me to be discouraged or depressed. He did not want me to feel unworthy or worthless. He loved me. If I was loved by the King of kings and Lord of lords, I had to be worth something. I was His and He was mine. That, I concluded, made me special in His sight. If I was good enough for Him, I was good enough for anyone. Not because of who I am, but because of who He is.

IF I WAS LOVED BY THE KING OF KINGS, I HAD TO BE WORTH SOMETHING.

I began to see that my children, not my duties, were my joy and hope. Shortly afterward the flowers came—a dozen red roses—followed by my great knight in his white station wagon. We all piled in and returned to our home in Portsmouth, Virginia, with eager anticipation of whatever the Lord would do next in our lives.

He has never let me down. He has never disappointed me. He knows my needs before I do. He even gives me the desires of my heart.

There's no room now in my life for self-pity. It distorts reality and can lead to endless trouble and doubts. Neither do I have room for dreams and fantasies, which can turn to nightmares. I have room only for Jesus. He fills my life completely. My will is His will. He is my happiness, my everything.

I was the product of the popular notion, "Get married and live happily ever after." When this didn't happen, I didn't know where to turn. But through this experience, the Holy Spirit showed me that I could always turn to Jesus. I can always count on Him. He will supply all my needs by His riches in glory—even my heart's desires. In doing so, God sometimes works through my husband, but often He chooses other ways. No matter what my need, He never fails. He's always there to forgive, to heal, to love—just as His Word promises: "My God shall supply all your need according to His riches in glory by Christ Jesus" (Philippians 4:19).

Dale Evans Rogers

LEARNING HUMILITY: PAINFUL BUT PRECIOUS

The wife of the late Roy Rogers, Dale Evans is one of America's most beloved personalities.

Actress, author, humanitarian, mother of nine, grandmother, and great-grandmother, she has been the recipient of many awards and honors. With Roy she is the holder of nine all-time box office records, and today she hosts her own television show on the Trinity Broadcasting Network.

She and Roy endeared themselves to my husband and me in many ways. Throughout their careers, Roy and Dale have represented honesty, decency, and faith in God and country. Experiencing the tragic loss of three children with all of their varied experiences gave them a message that the world desired to hear, and wherever they appeared, America's heart was with them.

Dale's Christian testimony is known around the world. One of the most dynamic statements I have ever heard was when Dale was speaking to a congressional wives' breakfast in Washington, D.C. She began her remarks with, "Ladies, God is real; I know, I have experienced Him." This was just a few weeks after the tragic loss of a second daughter, Debbie, in a church bus accident. Everyone knew her faith was real as she shared her victory through heartbreak.

At a luncheon where Dale was to speak later that day, there was "standing room only" as so many wanted to hear more and called friends to come. This same faith sustained Dale after the death of her beloved Roy in 1998. God has given her a ministry by first giving her a message—painful to learn, but precious to know and real to share. Here she shares a lesson on humility learned through the life and loss of her precious daughter Robin.

For forty-two years, God has been teaching me to be humble—to realize that of myself, my own ego, I am absolutely nowhere.

As you can imagine, this has been a difficult process for one who has been an extrovert since she was a small girl.

Often throughout my childhood I heard comments that helped to give me self-confidence: "Frances [my given name] is pretty; Frances is smart; Frances is talented; Frances will make her mark in the world." Consequently, the idea formed in my mind that I must live up to what was expected of me.

When I was eleven, I suffered a nervous breakdown and

spent the entire summer vacation in bed. I had skipped three grades in school and, thinking I was grown, had little to do with children my own age. I had a compulsion to be in everything, had to excel. You would think that that illness would have taught me a lesson, but I dreamed of being an actress, a ballerina, a singer, a writer—you name it.

At the age of ten, I accepted Jesus Christ as my Savior, but not as Lord of my life. Nothing ever quite satisfied me. Psalm 37:4 says, "Delight thyself also in the Lord; and he shall give thee the desires of thine heart." I knew nothing about delighting myself in Him. My own desires were paramount; never mind what the Lord wanted for me.

Not surprisingly, there was no peace in my heart. Somehow I felt everything depended upon me. Today I realize that everything—and I mean *everything*—depends on God.

At age thirty-seven, something happened that I could not control. God sent an "angel unaware" into my life in the person of Robin Elizabeth Rogers, the only child born to Roy and me. She was a pretty little blue-eyed blond Down's syndrome baby with a defective heart.

We had absolutely no place to go for help, except to God. I was devastated and heartbroken, for I had desperately wanted a little girl. I took refuge in God's Word, "Come unto me, all ye that labor and are heavy laden, and I will give you rest. Take my yoke upon you, and learn of me; for I am meek and lowly in heart: and ye shall find rest unto your souls. For my yoke is easy, and my burden is light" (Matthew 11:28–30).

Here I was, with a grown son, my Tom, three stepchildren, and a husband who was Number 1 in western box office with a huge following. It is quite clear that God was teaching me a valuable lesson.

I had asked Him at age thirty-five, shortly after my marriage to Roy, to take over my life completely, in every area. I wanted Him to use my life for His glory, not mine. In my heart, I believe our little Robin was the rod of correction He used to stop me dead in my tracks, to force me to take a hard look at where I had been and where I was going.

There is no scythe quite so sharp for scaling down pride like bringing a mentally and physically defective child into the world. It gets right to the root of the tree of pride.

As I went to Him in complete submission and humility, He began bestowing wonderful blessings in the midst of my anguish—peace in knowing that He would handle it, for I had given myself and my burden totally to Him. Deep within my heart, I knew that Jesus would chart and direct my path.

After Robin died, God enabled me to write *Angel Unaware*. People have asked me, "What has been the highest point of your life?" Without hesitation I reply, "The day Fleming H. Revell Company sent me a contract for publishing *Angel Unaware*, not for my glory, but for the glory of God."

To learn humility is painful, but precious. I have learned to humble myself in joyful recognition of the awesome power of God.

At the time of Robin's birth, no one admitted to having a Down's syndrome (mongoloid) child. Those little children were hidden from public view. The media mostly knew of our Robin's condition but in mercy and kindness never leaked it to the public. We lived then on a small ranch in Encino, California. We were highly publicized and to keep strangers out, we erected an electric gate. Even so, bus loads of curious sightseers would stop in front of our house, hoping to see us and our children.

When movie magazines sent reporters and photographers to our home, they kindly allowed us to edit any pictures taken of little Robin.

In vain we tried to find medical help for our baby, but we were told by a top pediatrician in the Mayo Clinic that it was useless to run here and there to specialists, for Down's syndrome could not be treated. We had the means to afford the best in the medical field, but nothing we could do would help. It was indeed a humbling situation.

HUMILITY AND DEPENDENCE ON GOD ARE NOT BESTOWED. THEY ARE LEARNED.

Had we not been committed Christians, this tragedy probably would have broken our marriage or our health. Gradually, the peace of the Lord took over and we knew that He would teach us what we needed to learn.

Humility and dependence on Him, you probably have discovered, are not bestowed. They are learned. The apostle Paul said, "I know both how to be abased, and I know how to abound: everywhere and in all things I am *instructed* both to be full and to be hungry, both to abound and to suffer need" (Philippians 4:12).

Someone asked me recently my definition of humility. I replied, "To be teachable." God is shaping us for eternity. He is knocking off our rough edges. I believe He wanted to make me teachable. When I "let go" of myself and asked Him to move into my life, I was on my way to learning obedience and humility.

I have had a hard schooling, but He has been faithful to

His promise to be with me in the process.

Some think humility is best pictured as a cowering, hand-wringing Uriah Heep. I believe humility is recognizing that "God so loved the world that He gave His only Son that whoever believes in Him will not perish but have everlasting life." Without Jesus, I do not believe there is any real abiding peace or joy in this life. Lucifer, the most beautiful of God's created heavenly beings, fell through pride. In his beauty, he wanted to be equal to or even greater than his Creator. One would think that he should have been grateful and happy to obey his Creator, thankful that God's plan for him was flawless.

How I wished I had understood this when I accepted Jesus as my Savior, but not my Lord.

My main regret in life is that I waited so long, made so many mistakes before "heeling to the Master."

Since my commitment to Christ in the spring of 1948, there have been tall, forbidding mountains to climb. But my Lord has been faithfully equipping me through prayers, study of His Word, and strength for the task. How He has tested me! I thank Him with all of my heart for teaching me the golden lesson of humility.

Joyce Rogers

SONLIGHT AT MIDNIGHT

Joyce Rogers has pioneered in the area of women's ministry. She has led in planning and has chaired nationwide women's conferences with thousands in attendance. She serves on the advisory board of Concerned Women for America as well as the Council of Biblical Womanhood, and has participated in the White House Meeting of Christian Women Leaders. She has also been elected president of the Southern Baptist Convention Ministers' Wives Conference for the year 2000. She is the author of The Wise Woman, The Secret of a Woman's Influence, *and* The Bible's Seven Secrets for Healthy Eating.

Her husband, three-time president of the Southern Baptist Convention, now pastors the historic Bellevue Baptist Church in Memphis, Tennessee, one of the world's largest churches. Joyce is first of all a homemaker—this is her greatest joy—yet she also enjoys a life as a leader of women, an author, speaker, singer, and world traveler.

She and her husband have led many trips to the Holy Land, and she sang the lead in the video production "From Israel With Love," which was filmed in Israel and hosted by Adrian.

Joyce is the mother of two sons and two daughters, and she has six grandchildren.

One of the greatest lessons I have learned from Joyce is not to ask God "Why?" but to ask Him "How?" As she shares her "greatest lesson," Joyce was obviously in the midst of one of the most difficult trials of her life. She doesn't have to share specific details to be helpful in relating tried-and-true principles that are meeting her present need—principles that will also help you meet your need.

God has enrolled me in an advanced course in His school of Christian living. The name of this difficult subject is "Waiting on God in Times of Darkness."

I showed up for the beginning class, "Times of Darkness 101," thirty-two years ago when our precious baby, Philip, was snatched into the arms of Jesus by sudden crib death. It was a lovely Mother's Day afternoon, and I was going to take a nap. Before lying down, I decided to check on the baby in the crib.

Philip looked blue. Frightened, I called for my husband. "Adrian! Come quick!"

Horror stricken, I asked, "Is he dead?"

Adrian quickly picked him up and said, "You stay here."

Our two other children, ages four and two years, were taking their naps. Adrian placed Philip's little body inside his coat and drove as fast as he could to the hospital. While he was gone, I quoted aloud those familiar words from the 23rd Psalm that I had learned as a child.

> The Lord is my shepherd, I shall not want...Yea, though I walk through the valley of the shadow of death, I will fear no evil: for thou art with me. Thy rod and thy staff they comfort me...

It seemed like an eternity before Adrian returned. I knew from the look on his face as he came up the sidewalk that Philip was gone. We had never lost a loved one. It felt dark, oh so dark, as we embraced each other. We had comforted others. We desperately needed comfort now.

Adrian and I made a few calls to family and friends. Soon they began to arrive, offering their love and sympathy.

Philip's funeral was held in our hometown sixty miles away. As we were leaving our house, the windows of our church next door were open, and we could hear the people singing, "No, never alone; no, never alone. He promised never to leave me. Never to leave me alone."

Although the darkness was never deeper, God's presence was never so real. What had until now been an easily sung song became a promise and a reality that I clung to with all my might: *"He promised never to leave me. Never to leave me alone."*

Even so, torrents of grief would repeatedly engulf me. Sometimes I literally held my hands up to God and said, "Lord, here, take my broken heart—it's too much for me to bear."

In time, I began learning to lean on the Lord. Someone

I didn't know sent me the following poem. In the ensuing years I have given many copies away. I memorized the words in those days. I treasure the message still.

Lean Hard

Child of My love, lean hard,
And let Me feel the pressure of thy care;
I know thy burden, child, I shaped it;
Poised it in Mine own hand, made no proportion
In its weight to thine unaided strength;

For even as I laid it on, I said,
I shall be near, and while he leans on Me,
This burden shall be Mine, not his;
So shall I keep My child within the circling arms
    of My own love.

Here lay it down, nor fear
To impose it on a shoulder which upholds
The government of worlds. Yet closer come;
Thou art not near enough; I would embrace thy care
So I might feel My child reposing on My breast.

Thou lovest Me? I knew it. Doubt not then
But loving Me, lean hard.

When we found Philip, there was no time to pray—no time to plead with God. He was gone.

The waiting on God came afterwards. This involved learning to lean hard on Him.

The waiting and leaning involved giving up my right to understand why. Through the strength of God's Holy Spirit and with the help of a Spirit-filled song by Ira Stanphill entitled "We'll Talk It Over," I handed my "right to understand why" over to God and was content to "wait for reasons 'til afterwhile."

The greatest lesson I learned in this "course" was praising the Lord at *all* times—even when it was dark. Not that this dark time was good—but I praised the God who was able to take even the bad things and work them together for good.

I discovered Psalm 63:3, which became my life's verse: "Because Your lovingkindness is better than life, my lips shall praise You." Then I was blessed by Psalm 34:1, "I will bless the Lord at all times; His praise shall continually be in my mouth." The Lord brought to mind Job 1:21, "The Lord gave, and the Lord has taken away; blessed be the name of the Lord."

I didn't feel like praising God, and I didn't want to fake my praise to God. That would produce no more than a sick grin. God showed me that He wanted me to *faith* my praise to Him. How I thank Him that it works. He also taught me just to *glance* at my circumstances but gaze upon Jesus. During this period of learning and waiting, He became my focus. I came to know Him in a way I never had before. In the words of Roy Hession, I learned that "it is enough to see Jesus and to go on seeing Him."

Then in a very practical lesson, God taught me to do what lay at hand—fold the diaper, sweep the floor, visit the sick, cook the meals, sing a song, study God's Word. Day by day He took me by the hand and led me out of darkness into His marvelous light.

But I told you that God had enrolled me in an *advanced* course in His school of Christian living—"Waiting on God in Times of Darkness." At this writing, I'm in a very difficult class, "Times of Darkness 401." In fact, it's the most difficult class in Christian living that I've ever experienced.

I don't want to fail. I need all the help I can get.

Because the situation is still being worked out, I do not have freedom to give the details. I would not want to cause any further grief or embarrassment to those involved, for they are precious to my husband and me. But I can testify that the experience, humanly speaking, is like the blackness of midnight!

When my baby died, I knew that I could either cast myself completely on God or turn away from Him. At that time I found Him to be more than sufficient for my need. My present hour of darkness has been worse than death. I've asked a thousand "whys," trying to figure it all out. But I come exhausted to the end of many a day knowing that only God holds the answer to the question why.

I'm grateful for the lessons I learned in "Times of Darkness 101." They have helped me to endure the present struggle. I've cast myself on my God over and over again. I know what it is to "lean hard" on Him, but I still struggle with giving up my "right to understand." Somehow it was so much easier to do when Philip died.

Oh, I've praised Him; and when I do, He brings such peace! I cannot describe the peace He brings in the midst of the storm—the joy with which He floods my soul when my eyes are filled with tears.

I find great comfort, too, in this poem by Janice Rogers Brock:

Joy Through My Teardrops

Joy through my teardrops, and gains through my losses
Beauty for ashes, and crowns for my crosses;
He binds my wounds, and He dries all my tears
Calms every storm and He conquers my fears.

He gives me hinds' feet to walk on high places
He floods my soul with His heavenly graces;
When I am weak then His strength makes me strong
I know I can trust Him, He's never been wrong.

Trials may come and temptations assail me
Though I may falter, He never will fail me;
So Satan, I bind you in His holy name
For at the cross Jesus' blood overcame!

When the doubt comes, when I'm lonely,
When my heart is sad;
I'll lift up mine eyes to my Savior above
And Jesus will make me glad.

When in my heart there is sadness and sorrow
Jesus has promised a brighter tomorrow;
Victory is mine; yes, it's already won.
I've only to claim it by faith in God's Son.

All of my cares I will cast down before Him
Even in trials my heart will adore Him;
He bears my burdens; He comforts my soul;
Oh, why should I worry when He's in control?

Lord, in the time of deep grief and emotion
I will yet serve You with constant devotion;
You have not failed me one step of the way,
That is the reason I'll trust You and say:

I will praise You! I will praise You!
Jesus Christ my King;
For You fill my heart with a song in the night.
Yes, You make my heart to sing!

I feel so helpless—so powerless! If there were only something I could do in my present situation. But I have had to find contentment in waiting on God.

Why does God take longer than we want Him to? He wants us to look to Him, to get to know Him better, to desire the Giver more than the gift. He also desires for us patience, endurance. I've discovered how very impatient I am. I want an answer *now*.

Andrew Murray once said, "If anyone is inclined to lose hope, because he does not have such patience, be encouraged. It is in the process of our weak and very imperfect waiting that God Himself by His hidden power strengthens us and works out in us the patience of the saints, the patience of Christ Himself. And if you sometimes feel as if patience is not your gift, then remember, it is God's gift."[1]

"IF YOU SOMETIMES FEEL AS IF PATIENCE IS NOT YOUR GIFT, THEN REMEMBER, IT IS GOD'S GIFT."

"In waiting on God it is important that we submit not because we are forced to, but because we lovingly and joyfully consent to be in the hands of our blessed Father. Patience then becomes our highest blessing and our highest grace. It honors God and gives Him time to have His way with us. It is the highest expression of our faith in His goodness and faithfulness. True patience is the losing of our self-will in His perfect will."[2]

In recent months my attention has been drawn to how many times we are called upon to wait. I've waited at the red light and the stop sign. I've waited at the doctor's office and in the hospital. There is even a room in some places called the "waiting room." I wait for my husband to come home for dinner, for my grown children to come for the holidays. I wait for the clerk in the department store. I wait in line at the bank. In fact, much of my life is spent waiting.

I've also learned that if I wait on others very long I get impatient. What will I do while I'm waiting? I've never even thought about it before now, but over the years I've developed a plan—things to keep me occupied and fill my waiting moments.

When I'm home there are a multitude of things to do— fold socks, write letters, make phone calls. The hardest time to wait is when I'm ready to go somewhere and I wonder if we'll be late.

One of the most effective things I've learned to do during those waiting times is to sit at my piano and play and sing praises to God. Sometimes I carry Scripture cards with me in the car. The seconds seem to fly as I memorize a phrase of God's Word while waiting at red lights. I almost always take my Bible to the doctor's office or to the beauty parlor.

Other times I'll take a book to read or some paper to write a letter. Recently I spent about twelve hours in the hospital, waiting for a grandbaby to be born. During that time I talked, read, wrote a letter, toured the gift shop several times, and prayed. I've written three books—much of them on airplanes, in hotel rooms, and under the dryer at the beauty parlor. This strategy helps me focus on God rather than my circumstances or difficulties.

Recently God revealed to me that the thing I did the least while I was waiting on others was *pray*. This was vividly brought to my attention when I found myself in one of the examining rooms at the doctor's office. I had forgotten to bring my Bible or a book. There was not even a magazine to read, or paper to write a letter. I thought to myself, *What a predicament, what a waste of precious time!*

Then came the inward rebuke: "You can always pray! You don't need pen or paper. You don't need a book or even the Bible to make contact with Me. Isolated from everyone, sitting on this examining table, you can have fellowship with Me—the source of all your needs. I am at the red light, under the dryer in the beauty parlor, in the waiting room at the hospital—yes, in the doctor's examining room. It doesn't have to be a waste of time as you are waiting on circumstances or waiting on others. If you could only recognize these times as opportunities to 'wait on Me,' it would revolutionize your life."

It is in times of waiting, whether planned or unplanned, that we come to recognize who He is—the One we are waiting for. He is a good God, filled with mercy and judgment. He has all power and wisdom. He is the source of our love and joy and peace. We must be still and wait to know His presence.

Andrew Murray said, "Seek not only the help or the gift, seek Him; wait for Him. Give God the glory by resting in Him, by trusting Him fully, by waiting patiently for Him. This patience honors Him greatly; it leaves Him as God on the throne to do His work; it yields self wholly into His hands. It lets God be God."[3]

I'm just beginning to remember this truth—waiting on others can remind us to wait on Him. Instead of becoming impatient, I find myself looking forward to those times. But I am so forgetful. I have a long way to go.

Surely one of the chief things God wants us to do while we wait on Him is to diligently search His Word. What delight I find in His truth. Psalm 18 is my favorite chapter in all of the Bible. I've gone back to it time and time again.

It is the story of how David waited on God in times of

darkness. He recounts those circumstances:

> The sorrows of death compassed me, and
>> The floods of ungodly men made me afraid.

> The sorrows of hell compassed me about:
>> The snares of death prevented me.

> The earth shook and trembled.

> The Lord also thundered in the heavens, and
>> The Highest gave his voice;
>> hail stones and coals of fire.

> The channels of waters were seen, and
>> The foundations of the world were
>> discovered at thy rebuke. (vv. 4,5,7,13,15)

The surroundings in David's life were extremely dark. There seemed to be no possible escape. But even before David tells of these dark days, he makes a declaration of love to God upon whom he was waiting and expecting deliverance:

> I will love thee, O Lord, my strength.

> The Lord is my rock, and my fortress, and my deliverer; my God, my strength, in whom I will trust; my buckler, and the horn of my salvation, and my high tower.

> I will call upon the Lord, who is worthy to be praised: so shall I be saved from mine enemies. (vv. 1–3)

David's love and trust never wavered. No matter what happened, he knew God's presence was with him. His faith was personal and intimate.

Then he recounted all the *distress* surrounding him. There were the threats of death, ungodly men, earthquake, and flood. It seemed as though not only men but God Him-self opposed him. But in his distress he cried out to his God:

> In my distress I called upon the Lord, and cried unto my God: he heard my voice out of his temple, and my cry came before him, even into his ears. (v. 6)

David knew God heard. But deliverance didn't come. There was a *delay*. Then more distress. In fact, darkness set in. But in the midst of the darkness we see someone flying on a cherub on the wings of the wind (v. 10). Can it be? Yes. It is God Himself! He was there in the darkness. He was in control. In fact, "darkness was under His feet" (v. 9).

Then things got worse. God thundered in the heavens; He sent out His arrows; He shot out lightnings—the floods broke loose. All seemed lost and then—oh then, *deliverance* finally came.

> He sent from above,
> He took me,
> He drew me out of many waters.
>
> He delivered me...
> He brought me forth also into a large place;
> He delivered me, because he delighted in me.
> (vv. 16,17,19)

And then:

> The Lord rewarded me according to my righteous-ness; according to the cleanness of my hands hath he recompensed me. (v. 20)

The darkness lifted!

> For thou wilt light my candle: the Lord my God will enlighten my darkness. (v. 28)

It seemed as if a whole army had marched against David and he was up against a brick wall. He declared:

> For by thee I have run through a troop; and by my God have I leaped over a wall. (v. 29)

I believe I can hear David singing, "Hallelujah, Hallelujah!" Oh, I can't understand why God delayed His deliverance, but "His way is perfect" (v. 30). Oh, the praise and thanksgiving that followed!

> For who is God save the Lord? Or who is a rock save our God? It is God that girdeth me with strength, and maketh my way perfect. He maketh my feet like hinds' feet, and setteth me upon my high places. (v. 31–33)

And besides all that:

> Thou hast also given me the shield of thy salvation: and thy right hand hath holden me up, and thy gentleness hath made me great. (v. 35)

And more!

> Thou hast enlarged my steps under me, that my feet did not slip. (v. 36)

Deliverance hasn't come for me yet:

But my God
  I will love You

You are my strength
  My rock
  My fortress

You are my high tower.

Oh my God
  I run into You to hide.

Oh God, it is so dark
    I cannot see.

Please hold my hand
    and lead me through
    this darkness.

Take my hand.
    We can run through the troop
    and leap over this wall.

Hallelujah! Hallelujah!

There's nothing I can do, Lord. I wait on You. Thank You for *Sonlight at midnight!*

Edith Schaeffer

STAYING IN GOD'S FOGS WHILE TRUSTING HIM

Edith Schaeffer, with her late husband, Dr. Francis Schaeffer, co-founded the well-known Christian community in Switzerland, L'Abri Fellowship. The work of L'Abri began in the midst of their own young family in 1955 in the village of Huemoz, Switzerland. Today L'Abri has six branches around the world—one each in Switzerland, England, Holland, Sweden, and Korea, and two in the United States.

Born in China of missionary parents, who were serving with the China Inland Mission under Hudson Taylor, Edith is the author of numerous books on a variety of topics. A resident of Rochester, Minnesota, she has four children, and many grandchildren and great-grandchildren. She is active with L'Abri in Rochester, and is a speaker and counselor in the United States and abroad.

The account of Edith's lesson of trust cannot help but encourage faith that God can meet our every need and that He may choose to meet our need "just in the nick of time."

Perhaps you have discovered, as I have, that memory needs to be sharpened if we are going to learn valuable lessons in life.

As I walk through my memories, I realize that it was always during "impossible" moments—when the brick wall ahead of me was without a "door" in sight—that I learned my most important lessons.

I am in my eighties now, but still very sensitive to the fact that I am *far* from being a "finished product" and that I have much to learn—and that even the *same* lessons need to be learned over and over again.

No doubt you have discovered, as have I, that we do make progress in our learning. But there is never any room for smugness or pride!

Back in 1955 (you can read the whole story in the book *L'Abri*), my husband, Francis, and I were in one of our most "impossible" positions. We had two-year-old Franky, with polio, and thirteen-year-old Susan, with rheumatic fever. Floods and avalanches had filled our downstairs with mud, which had taken us a week to fight with shovels and sandbags. In addition, we were being evicted from our home.

Although we had lived in the Swiss village of Champery for more than five years, on February 14 we received two sheets of paper from the village gendarmery (police) notifying us that we had six weeks to get out because "You have had a religious influence on the village of Champery."

In the midst of our prayer about what to do next, as a family with four children and no money, we were told that the only way to appeal the edict was to find another house, in another village, in another canton, and to make arrangements to live in it. The sheaf of papers to be filled out for the appeal had spaces to put the address of a house and the signature of someone who would declare that we indeed had made arrangements to buy or rent it. We were given only five days to make such an arrangement.

We had been looking in villages that we could reach by train, when a Czechoslovakian couple we knew stopped us in distress, and I was pressed into accompanying them to a hospital miles away because of an imminent, premature birth. Having given up the search, Fran had gone back to our own chalet to pack. We had planned to leave Switzerland if we could not find a house in another village.

I spent a sleepless night in the Lausanne hospital, then called my husband in the morning. "Oh, Fran, I'm going to go on looking. If I find a chalet today, will you come tomorrow to look at it with me and fill out the papers?"

"Yes, if you do...though I doubt that you will," he replied.

This fired me with determination to find something. I prayed, but with spiritual pride that *I* had not given up and *I* had faith enough to keep on.

That day I felt like a lost child gazing wistfully at other children safe in their homes and was close to tears as I tramped through the snow in Villars. Suddenly I saw a "for rent" sign on a weather-beaten, rustic chalet. I inquired into the whereabouts of the owner, and walked on, another mile and a half, to a school in Arveyes where the owner was headmistress. I planned to inspire her to compassion by a story so appealing that she could not resist renting the chalet to us at a very reasonable price. I was shown into her parlor.

This dignified lady quoted the rent, then went on to mention a grand piano, antiques, Persian rugs, and the many other features of the chalet. But the rental price blurred the rest out, and I burst into tears. The price for *one month* was what we had paid for a *year* in Chalet Bijou.

I dabbed my eyes with my handkerchief. "Oh, excuse me, I don't usually break down like this. But I had no sleep last night, assisting at the birth of a baby. Now I have to find a chalet within an hour, or we'll have to leave Switzerland."

She looked at me pityingly, and I read in her eyes, "This person is a little off her head; better ease her out of here." And before I knew it, I had been gently propelled to the front door, and I was outside!

Feeling I had made an utter fool of myself, I walked slowly down her path into deeper snow. I was filled with a sudden realization of how God saw me and began to pray, "Oh, heavenly Father, forgive me for insisting on my own will today. I really do want to want Your will. Please help me to be sincere in this. Forgive me for closing the door on the possibility of Your having a totally different plan for the next step of our lives. Oh God, I am willing to live in city slums, if it is Your will."

I felt a surge of trust in the God of Elijah, Daniel, and Joseph and continued, "But God, if You want us to stay in Switzerland, in these mountains, I know *You* are able to find a house, and lead me to it in the *next half hour*. Nothing is impossible to You."

I reached the main street of Villars just as a chattering, laughing crowd was returning from skiing and crowding into the tearooms. I kept my eyes on the snowy pavement, not wanting to see anyone, as my eyes were red with weeping.

Suddenly I heard my name. *"Madame Schaeffer, avez-vous trouve quelque chose?"*

I looked up to see Monsieur Gabuz, a real estate dealer to whom we had talked days before. He had not shown us even one chalet, because he said everything he had was "deluxe" and far above our price range. I was surprised that he remembered my name.

I answered, *"Non, Monsieur Gabuz...rien."*

"Hop in," he said. "I think I have something that might interest you. Would you mind living in Huemoz?"

"Huemoz, where's that?" I asked.

We drove on down the mountainside, fog blotting out the view, and weariness dampening my enthusiasm. The car stopped beside a postal bus stop sign and a mail box. Climbing out, we went up a pair of log steps buried in the snow, opened a gate, and crunched our way to the front of the chalet. It was tightly shuttered with full-length balconies. We walked into a musty dark room, and Monsieur Gabuz opened shutters while explaining that it had not been lived in for a long time. There I was, in a chalet within the half hour, not because I had had wisdom or cleverness to find it, but because God had answered my prayer. This I believed to be the *only* explanation.

I arranged to meet Monsieur Gabuz the next morning with Fran. Then I remembered something.

"Oh, Monsieur Gabuz, I forgot to ask...how much is the rent?"

"Oh, it's not for rent," he called out of the car, "it's for sale." Then he shot up the road.

"For sale," I repeated to myself dully. "For sale! We have no money, and even if we were millionaires, *who* would buy a house in a country without a permit to live there?"

This seemed the last straw to me. I was feeling sick with exhaustion from sleeplessness and the emotional struggle. As I rode down on the bus, and up on the train to Champery, I began to review the last days and hours. It seemed that the markers of answered prayer definitely indicated that God *had* been leading up to this point. Before I arrived at Chalet Bijou in Champery, I was convinced that God had given me a clear sign and that we must go back the next day.

When I arrived, Fran gave me the most recent news. "Berne has given us an extension. We may stay in Switzerland until the matter has been studied, but Sion will give *no* extension of time, and we have to be out of this chalet and this village and this canton by midnight March 31. Franky's doctor even telephoned to tell them that the children should not be moved at this time for health reasons. But Sion would give no extension unless we and the children would sign a paper saying that we would not talk about religious matters to people in or outside of our chalet!"

That night I prayed again. One can't put an hour of talking to God in a paragraph, but it is important to say that it *was* an hour, not a sentence. As I asked for God's guidance about the chalet, which had seemed such an exciting answer to prayer that afternoon and now seemed so impossible, I determined to ask the owner to change his mind and rent it. But suddenly I felt flooded with assurance that nothing is impossible to God. My prayer changed, startling me as I asked, "Oh, please show us Your will about this house tomorrow, and if we are to *buy* it, send us a sign that will be clear enough to convince Fran as well as me; send us $1,000 before ten o'clock tomorrow morning."

The following morning, the postman—on skis—handed us three letters. We opened these on the train. One was from Paris, one from Belgium, and the third was from a man and his wife in Ohio. They had been following our work with interest and prayer for quite some time. However, they had never given financial help to our work, nor were they wealthy. Mrs. Salisbury wrote:

I have a story that will interest you. Three months ago Art received an unexpected sum of money. His company had decided to pay insurance premiums for all their employees, retroactive for those who had worked there a number of years. Our thought was to invest in a little house, which we would rent. As we looked over a very likely house, I suddenly saw signs of termites in the beams. "Look, Art, doesn't that remind you of the verse in Matthew, 'Lay not up for yourselves treasures upon earth, where moth and rust corrupt, and where thieves break through and steal: but lay up for yourselves treasures in heaven, where neither moth nor rust corrupt, and where thieves do not break through nor steal'? Art, would you be willing to take this money and invest it literally in heaven? Would you be willing to give it to the Lord's work somewhere?" He replied, "Yes, Helen, I would."

For months, we have been asking God to show us what He would have us do with this money. Tonight we have come to a definite decision; both of us feel certain that we are meant to send you this money...to buy a house somewhere that will always be open to young people.

The amount of money was exactly $1,000!

I poured out the story of my prayer and the fact that the house was for *sale*. As the train arrived at Ollon, Fran and I were convinced that God was leading us to *buy* Chalet les Melezes. The perfect timing of the arrival of the letter and of my certainty at the moment I had prayed for that money were amazing. Mrs. Salisbury's statement that the money was for buying a house "that will always be open to young people" was a prophecy of our future work that neither she nor we could have known at the time.

A short time later we stepped off the bus at the bus stop that was to become familiar to a variety of people in coming years. That morning it was deserted, with an empty house above it, and another enormous empty house at one side. We were soon looking through the chalet to see what God had chosen for us, with the feeling that we were not making a choice at all.

"Yes, we'll take it" was easy to say that morning with our excitement and assurance over the unmistakable sign from God. When the agent told us that we needed a $10,000 mortgage and would need $7,000 cash, we didn't bat an eyelash...not then. We were in a hurry to fill in the sheets of paper and send off our appeal.

We went immediately to Lausanne to see a lawyer, the police, and a notary. The Chief helped us to fill in the papers properly. We learned that we had found the chalet just in time; another day would have been too late!

Arrangements were made to make the promissory payment the following day, and binding papers were signed. We had paid 8,000 francs (about $2,000), which had come in surprisingly small amounts, and said we would pay another $5,000 by May 31 or forfeit all that had been paid, plus a lot more! This rigid and binding agreement was frightening to sign. The clarity of guidance was followed by impossibility. In other words, a brick wall with *no* door seemed to be where the choice led, but signposts behind us gave fresh assurance!

The greatest lesson I was learning then is one that I am *still* learning. We never become a finished product. Isaiah wrote:

> Who among you fears the Lord and obeys the word of his servant? Let him who walks in the dark, who has no light, trust in the name of the Lord and rely on his God. But now, all you who light fires and provide yourselves with flaming torches, go, walk in the light of your fires and of the torches you have set ablaze. This is what you shall receive from my hand: You will lie down in torment [or sorrow] (Isaiah 50:10,11).

Throughout life, we must discover time after time *when* we have crossed the fine line between trusting and relying upon God and lighting our own fires (forcing our own plans).

I learned to be alert and sensitive to my own danger of stepping *out of the fog* to ignite my own sparks. Fires so often seem more secure than staying in God's fogs and trusting Him.[1]

Joni Eareckson Tada

IT'S CALLED "UNITY"

In 1967 Joni Eareckson broke her neck in a diving accident that left her paralyzed from the shoulders down. Learning to draw with a pencil held between her teeth during her
two years of rehabilitation, she is now an internationally
known mouth artist.

She is recognized by her first name in many countries,
largely as a result of her twenty-six best-selling books, including her autobiography Joni. A full-length feature film of her
life, in which she played herself, has been seen all over the
world, and her inspirational radio program is heard daily
over more than eight hundred broadcast outlets by millions
of listeners.

Joni has served on the National Council on Disability to
which she was appointed by President Reagan in 1987. She
has been chairman of the Christian Council on Persons with
Disabilities, a national consortium of Christian ministries
serving disabled persons, and has served on several advisory
groups and boards, including the Lausanne Committee for
World Evangelization.

She is the founder and president of Joni and Friends, which provides an information and referral program, workshops, audio-visual materials, and the Christian Fund for the Disabled, a financial assistance program.

Residing in California with her husband, Ken Tada, a high school social studies teacher, Joni travels extensively on speaking tours throughout the United States and many foreign countries. She holds an honorary Doctor of Humanities degree from Gordon College and an honorary doctorate from Columbia University, and has been chosen to serve as honorary chairman of the Sino-American Higher Education Center for Special Education in Jiangxi, China. She is the recipient of the American Academy of Achievement's Golden Plate Award and the Courage Award of the Courage Rehabilitation Center. She was named "Churchwoman of the Year" in 1993 by the Religious Heritage Foundation and "Layperson of the Year" by the National Association of Evangelicals.

Joni's radiant smile, happy spirit, and sensitivity to the needs of others are a great encouragement to Bill and me and all who have opportunity to meet her. The following account reveals this sensitivity and her special insight into other people.

It's not often that you see a parable lived out before your eyes. But it happened to me on the spring morning I went with my husband, Ken, to the Los Angeles Special Olympics.

Band music, colorful banners, and flags were everywhere. Scattered across the infield were teams of mentally handicapped young people with their friends and families. Everyone was on tiptoe with excitement, waiting for the games to begin.

I positioned my wheelchair near the grandstand so I could get a good view of Ken who was serving as track and field coordinator. I spotted him at the far end of the track in his red warm-ups and visor, with whistle and clipboard. He was helping to pin numbers on the back of each contestant.

After a few minutes, it was time for the fifty-yard dash to begin. Ken blew his whistle to signal for the contestants to line up at their starting blocks. A Down's syndrome girl with thick glasses and a big smile jumped up and down clapping her hands. A short, stocky, mentally handicapped boy in baggy gray shorts kept kicking the dirt. A tall, gangly young man waved to his family in the stands. These kids could barely contain their excitement.

Ken quieted the runners. There was a moment of stillness and then a "bang" from the starting gun. Off they sprinted—six contestants bobbing and weaving down the track to the wild cheers of the crowd. Some skipped, a few stumbled, but each one raced, as best he could, toward the other end of the track.

Suddenly, one of the runners—a Down's syndrome boy in a blue T-shirt—skipped the curb of the track and began running toward his friends in the infield. Ken blew his whistle, waved and called to the boy, trying to direct him back to the track. It was no use—this was one contestant determined to race away from the finish line.

At that point one of the other runners, the girl with thick glasses, noticed the boy's detour. She stopped a few yards from the finish line while the other contestants raced past her. She called to her fellow runner in the infield and shouted, "Hey, come this way!"

When the boy in the blue T-shirt heard his friend's voice, he stopped and turned around. The girl with glasses waved and called again, "This is the right way...come back!"

He stood there and looked around, somewhat confused. Exasperated, but with a smile on her face, she ran toward him and gave him a big hug when she caught up with him. They linked elbows and together got back on the track, finishing the race arm-in-arm. The last to cross the finish line, the two contestants were hugged by their friends who had finished long before them.

The entire crowd was standing at that point, enraptured by the poignancy of the scene. Some clapped, many cheered, but most, like me, sat in wonder, trying hard to hold back the tears. We knew we had witnessed something special.

That night, Ken and I sat at our kitchen table talking about the day's events. He shook his head and smiled as he sipped his hot chocolate. "I've been track and field coordinator there for many years," he sighed, set down his mug, and then continued, "but nothing has touched me like that little girl today. She set aside her goal in order to help a confused friend reach the finish line."

We had seen a parable lived out before our eyes that day. And it didn't take much to find a verse from Scripture to match the meaning behind that unique race.

Ken flipped to Romans 15 and found the exact words:

> We who are strong ought to bear with the failings of the weak and not to please ourselves. Each of us should please his neighbor for his good, to build him up... May the God who gives endurance and encouragement give you a spirit of unity among yourselves as you follow Christ Jesus (Romans 15:1,2,5).

We closed the Bible and sat there a long moment. "Each of us should please his neighbor for his good, to build him up…" I thought of all the times I failed to set aside my goals long enough to help a weaker friend in need. I thought of all the times I had watched a fellow believer get off the right track, get lost and spiritually confused, and yet I kept right on going. I recalled times when the Lord told me to forget my carefully outlined agenda in order to help someone else, some friend unsure of where to go. Sadly, I often neglected to do so for fear of not "winning," of not crossing my personal "finish line."

And I'm not the only one. Unfortunately, there are few who, when they become Christians, automatically begin "looking out for the interests of others," as Scripture puts it. That's why it's no surprise that the Bible also says we need to be "trained in godliness." And as we "press on toward the prize of the high calling of knowing Christ Jesus," we must remember that there are others running the race with us, even in the lanes next to us.

WINNING ISN'T IMPORTANT, BUT HOW WE RUN THE RACE IS.

The Lord Jesus doesn't seem as preoccupied as we do with "winning." In fact, as Ken reminded me, the object behind Special Olympics games is simply to encourage everyone to finish the race. It matters little if a contestant comes in first, second, third, or even last. Every runner is surrounded by a grandstand of witnesses, cheering and applauding the efforts of all. Winning isn't important, but how we run the race is. And we are to run it "bearing with the failings of the weak."

Since that spring morning, I've seen many parables come to life before my eyes, but none so poignant and powerful as watching those two handicapped runners cross the finish line arm-in-arm. If I want the Lord Jesus to be glorified in my life, I must run the race not to please myself, but to please the Lord—and that will often mean taking time to stop and put my arm around a weaker friend. Romans 15 has a word for it. And if you asked the handicapped girl and her friend, they might even say it.

It's called "unity."

Vonette Zachary Bright

In Search of Identity

As the publisher and I were talking about this project, I thought he was going to let me off the hook. But no, he wanted a story from me as well. So I went back into my memories, and this particular lesson is one I felt led to share. Whenever I have shared these principles, women have told me it meant a lot to them.

I am a very practical-minded person. I look for reasons, answers, and applications. This is why I am so excited about this book. So many times we forget that the Bible is God's textbook to mankind. It contains truths and principles to help us solve or cope with every problem we can face, though we are prone to first look everywhere else for answers. It is in the Bible that God tells us how to relate to Him, to each other, to our spouse, and to our children.

Fortunately for me there were women I admired who directed me to the Bible for answers when dishes, diapers, *dust, and drudgery tempted me to escape to what seemed so much more glamorous.*

Here's how I found my identity which put life and priorities in focus for me.

With Campus Crusade for Christ staff in more than 180 countries, my husband and I do a great deal of traveling. Our ministry responsibilities usually require us to visit each continent every year, where we meet with staff, other Christian leaders, and government officials.

Around the globe, I have encountered the poor and the rich, the illiterate and the highly educated, the discouraged and the greatly motivated. I have met people of all ages in many different cultures and stations in life. I have observed their lifestyles and the way they express themselves and relate to each other. All this has taught me that people around the world are much alike, separated only by language and culture.

Modern travel and communication have shown us that, though our cultures are different, there is a thread of commonality in all of us: We have similar needs for fulfillment; we have unanswered questions in our quest for identity.

In my lifetime I have seen major changes in our value system that have had a dramatic effect on what people believe will provide maximum fulfillment. As a college student in the late 1940s, when family was still important, I was encouraged to prepare for a career—in case I needed it, and for the pleasure of culture, knowledge, and understanding.

At that time, women in large numbers had experienced

the liberty of working outside the home in defense plants to aid the war effort. As the post-war years rolled by, they were taught that fulfillment came in achievement and that their maximum potential was to be found in the market-place where they would have visible leadership and identity. As a result, even more women sought careers, only to discover frustration and disillusionment.

In recent years I have seen the mood of women in the United States come full circle from an era when the family was most important, through the disillusionment of the '60s and '70s, then through the '80s when marriage and family once again became of greater value, though coupled with the woman's career. The mother of the '90s, according to the December 4, 1989, issue of *TIME* Magazine, is returning home to care for her family if it is at all economically possible.

Often, in the very moment of achievement, there is no satisfaction. Have you ever felt empty or unfulfilled at the point of accomplishment as though something inside were saying, "So what? Big deal"? The rewards of achievement and visible leadership are rarely enough.

The road to achievement often is a struggle for power—all the power you can get. But the Word of God—and even secular psychologists—tell us that there is much greater fulfillment in giving than receiving. Thus the steps we often take toward achievement are leading us in the opposite direction of fulfillment.

In many countries and cultures, today's woman is trying to stretch herself into a number of roles at one time. Perhaps for economic necessity or personal achievement, she may have her own career; she must be a perfect lover and companion, a good mother, devoted to social causes with perfect calmness and composure, and she must *achieve* in each area. The result, doctors tell us, is that more women are suffering from heart attacks and stress-related illnesses than ever before.

I have learned that lasting happiness is found in relation-ships, not achievements. What happens if the function or circumstances in which a woman places her identity changes? If identity is in *career* and that fails, where is her identity? If identity is in *marriage* and that fails, then what? If identity is in *children*, where is her identity when they leave home? We need to place our identity in that which will not change.

The great French physicist and philosopher, Blaise Pascal, is well known for having said, "There is a God-shaped vacuum in the heart of every person which cannot be satisfied by any created thing, but only by God, the Creator, made known through Jesus Christ." People think they can find identity in things of this world, but these can all change. I believe a re-warding, sustaining lifestyle is that which is found in a personal faith and trust in Jesus Christ and in being obe-dient to whatever He desires us to do. We must place our identity in the One who will not change.

WE MUST PLACE OUR IDENTITY IN THE ONE WHO WILL NOT CHANGE.

Identity in Jesus Christ is the glue that has held my life together. Although I grew up in the church and appreciate my religious background, God was not a reality in my life. Life was routine and happiness depended upon circumstances. Into my confusion walked Bill Bright—handsome, moral, and successful. We had a whirlwind romance but waited three years to be married.

During that time, Bill was growing in his faith. I was getting farther away from mine. I decided he had become a religious fanatic, and he detected that I was not a Christian. Since we were idealistic enough to seek agreement on every major issue, we questioned our coming marriage.

To make a long story short, I was very much impressed with Bill's friends at Hollywood Presbyterian Church. He introduced me to Dr. Henrietta Mears, director of Christian education, who compared the reality of knowing God personally to performing a chemistry lab experiment. Since I minored in chemistry in college, it made sense to me to add the person of Jesus Christ to the ingredients of faith I already knew. I received Jesus Christ as my personal Savior. As a result, God has become a vital reality in my life giving me identity and direction.

Early in our marriage, Bill and I committed ourselves totally to Christ as a couple. God blessed us with achievement.

My teaching career was successful, and a course of study written for my master's project was selected to be taught in the Los Angeles public schools and syndicated throughout the United States. God gave Bill the idea for a Christian movement that would help reach the world for Christ and help bring our nation back to the fundamentals on which it was established.

I chose to work with him so we could build and achieve God's purpose for our lives together.

I used my experience in teaching to help write our staff training manuals. Together we have influenced two human beings—our sons Zac and Brad—to become accountable, responsible, godly young men who are both now in Christian ministry. Through them and our thousands of full-time and associate Campus Crusade staff, we are touching tens of millions of lives around the world with the life-changing message of Christ's love and forgiveness.

There were times of adjustments, hard work, great concern, and many joys that have given me a message to share and enable me to minister to the lives of others today.

In examining my life and analyzing my identity, I realize that God has given me role models in women whom I have admired and sought to emulate. Some of these are mentioned in Scripture. My favorite among Bible women is Esther, the queen of the Persian Empire who risked her life to save her people, the Jews.

Another model is Catherine Booth, wife of Salvation Army founder William Booth. She was the mother of eight children, yet maintained a vital personal ministry. No doubt some said, "Catherine, your children are going to go astray while you maintain such an active ministry." But she lived a godly life and was obedient to what God called her to do, and all eight children entered some phase of Christian ministry. Catherine's story exemplifies that a mother can indeed have a ministry while keeping her home life a very high priority.

What about some more recent models? Mother Teresa, the Albanian nun who received worldwide recognition (including the Nobel Prize) for her mission to the poor and dying in Calcutta, is an inspiring model to many. When asked by someone how she dealt with so much failure, her reply was, "God has not called me to be successful. He has called me to be faithful."

Henrietta Mears, a single woman who invested her life in Christian education, is another. She influenced many in her lifetime, including Bill and me and more than four hundred young men who entered the ministry as pastors of many different denominations.

Let me tell you of a couple of "ordinary women" who, in addition to my mother, served as role models to me.

Mrs. Louis H. Evans, Sr., the wife of one of America's most outstanding Presbyterian pastors, was the mother of four children. She totally devoted herself as a wife and mother to her family who are making their mark on the world.

The other woman was a beautiful and gifted school teacher who married a rancher. At age sixteen she had committed her life totally to Christ, telling Him that for the rest of her life she wanted to do only what would glorify God the most.

Her life on the 5,000-acre ranch in rural Oklahoma was hard. She gave birth to eight children, one of whom died shortly after birth. Her home was the rural entertainment center for the community, and at meal times she was never sure how many people she would be serving in addition to her family.

Her children recall how she spent time reading her Bible each morning and evening and sang hymns as she went about her work. The most Christlike person in the community anyone could recall, she lived thirty-five years with a non-Christian husband, then lived another thirty-five years with him after he received Christ.

She was extremely ill most of the nine months that she carried her seventh child. There was little hope from the doctor that she would live to give birth to the child. She prayed earnestly, promising the Lord that she would commit this child to Him and His service, if He would let her live to give birth.

This woman was truly a Proverbs 31 woman whose 109

members of her family, including children, grandchildren, great-grandchildren, and great-great grandchildren, made their way to her bedside to express their love and appreciation before her death at age ninety-three. All of them have risen up to call her "blessed." This woman continues to have a great influence, perhaps even in your life, for she was my husband's mother, Mary Lee Bright.

All of these women had one thing in common—their identity in Christ. Inspired by the models in my life, I decided to follow Christ. I learned to apply the Scriptures to daily living, not content to declare one thing and live another, or to export that which didn't work at home.

Each of us is a special person with unique skills, gifts, and capabilities. Each of us has a unique sphere of influence. Whoever we are and wherever we go, we are going to be a role model for someone. The question is, what kind?

The greatest lesson I have learned is that my significance, fulfillment, maximum potential, and identity come not from achievement, recognition, or position. They come from a relationship with a Person—the most remarkable Person of all time, One whose life literally changed the course of history: our Lord Jesus Christ. I desire to have others know that lasting identity, too.

Bringing It All Together

There you have it—twenty-three women who are living lives of significance, making a personal contribution in their sphere of influence. Some are more visible in their influence than others, but that does not matter. What does matter is that they are taking advantage of the opportunities they have to help make the world a better place in which to live. There is a thread in each experience that is common to all. They each have found peace and direction in their heart that enables them to reach out to touch the lives of others.

Pondering the content of this book, I have asked myself, "What is missing?" I am reminded of a woman in Oklahoma City who came to me after I had spoken to a women's luncheon. "Thank you," she said, "I now know why my friend has been bringing me to these luncheons month after month. I decided if there were not some specific directions given to me today, I would not attend again. We have heard women tell inspiring experiences of how their lives have been changed, but none has been explicit as to how I might experience the reality of God in my life. Today, you have given me the answer—and I believe I have begun the adventure I've been hearing about."

This woman's statement is typical of what has been repeated many times to me around the world. It was true in my own experience. I had gone to church all of my life. I am so grateful for my church background; it helped me stand strong when some of my friends were disintegrating morally around me. I had endeavored to live as much as I could (in my own strength) according to the teachings of the Bible. I am grateful for pastors, Sunday school teachers, and godly individuals who invested their lives in mine. Yet, God was not a reality in my life.

I once discussed this with my pastor, the late Dr. Louis Evans, at that time minister-at-large for the Presbyterian Church USA. He explained that it does not make any difference *when* a person receives Christ—as a child, a young adult, or a senior adult—but it is important that he *has* received Christ and that he knows for sure that he is rightly related to God. He went on to explain that it is impossible to grow in your personal faith until you have the assurance that Jesus Christ is in control of your life.

But how can you be sure you are rightly related to God? I know no better way to share with you than what was made clear to me and what the woman heard in Oklahoma City.

Because I searched so long for a definite understanding, I have determined never to speak without an attempt to make clear how an individual can know God personally. The same is true of this book. Every one of these women would want to share with you in personal conversation, if possible, how the dimension of personal faith in Jesus Christ has allowed them to find true peace and fulfillment.

Are you looking for answers? Would you like to know God personally? If you are still searching, let me share four principles[1] that, if applied, will enable you to know the reality of God in your life.

1 GOD LOVES YOU, AND CREATED YOU TO KNOW HIM PERSONALLY.

While the Bible is filled with assurances of God's love, perhaps the most telling verse is John 3:16:

> For God so loved the world, that He gave His only begotten Son, that whoever believes in Him should not perish, but have eternal life.

God not only loves each of us enough to give His only Son for us; He desires that we come to know Him personally:

> Now this is eternal life; that they may know you, the only true God, and Jesus Christ, whom you have sent (John 17:3, NIV).

What, then, prevents us from knowing God personally?

2 MEN AND WOMEN ARE SINFUL AND SEPARATED FROM GOD, SO WE CANNOT KNOW HIM PERSONALLY OR EXPERIENCE HIS LOVE.

We were all created to have fellowship with God; but, because of mankind's stubborn self-will, we chose to go our own independent way and fellowship with God was broken. This self-will, characterized by an attitude of active rebellion or passive indifference, is evidence of what the Bible calls sin.

> All have sinned and fall short of the glory of God (Romans 3:23).

The Bible also tells us that "the wages of sin is death" (Romans 6:23), or spiritual separation from God. When we are in this state, a great gulf separates us from God, because He cannot tolerate sin. People often try to bridge the gulf by doing good works or devoting themselves to religious practices, but the Bible clearly teaches that there is only one way to bridge this gulf...

3 JESUS CHRIST IS GOD'S ONLY PROVISION FOR OUR SIN. THROUGH HIM ALONE WE CAN KNOW GOD PERSONALLY AND EXPERIENCE HIS LOVE.

God's Word records three important facts to verify this principle: 1) Jesus Christ died in our place; 2) He rose from the dead; and 3) He is our only way to God:

God demonstrates His own love toward us, in that while we were yet sinners, Christ died for us (Romans 5:8).

Christ died for our sins...He was buried...He was raised on the third day, according to the Scriptures... He appeared to Peter, then to the twelve. After that He appeared to more than five hundred... (1 Corinthians 15:3–6).

Jesus said to him, "I am the way, and the truth, and the life; no one comes to the Father, but through Me" (John 14:6).

Thus, God has taken the loving initiative to bridge the gulf that separates us from Him by sending His Son, Jesus

Christ, to die on the cross in our place to pay the penalty for our sin. But it is not enough just to know these truths…

4 WE MUST INDIVIDUALLY RECEIVE JESUS CHRIST AS SAVIOR AND LORD; THEN WE CAN KNOW GOD PERSONALLY AND EXPERIENCE HIS LOVE.

John 1:12 records:

> As many as received Him, to them He gave the right to become children of God, even to those who believe in His name.

What does it mean to "receive Christ"? The Scriptures tell us that we receive Christ through faith—not through "good works" or religious endeavors:

> By grace you have been saved through faith; and that not of yourselves, it is the gift of God; not as a result of works, that no one should boast (Ephesians 2:8,9).

We're also told that receiving Christ means to personally invite Him into our lives:

> [Christ is speaking] Behold, I stand at the door and knock; if anyone hears My voice and opens the door, I will come in to him (Revelation 3:20).

Thus, receiving Christ involves turning to God from self …and trusting Christ to come into our lives to forgive our sins and to make us the kind of people He wants us to be.

If you are not sure whether you have ever committed your life to Jesus Christ, I encourage you to do so—today!

Here is a suggested prayer that has helped millions of men and women around the world express faith in Him and invite Him into their lives:

> Lord Jesus, I want to know You personally. Thank You for dying on the cross for my sins. I open the door of my life and receive You as my Savior and Lord. Thank You for forgiving my sins and giving me eternal life. Take control of the throne of my life. Make me the kind of person You want me to be.

If this prayer expresses the desire of your heart, why not pray it now? If you mean it sincerely, Jesus Christ will come into your life, just as He promised in Revelation 3:20. He keeps His promises! And there is another key promise I suggest you write indelibly in your mind:

> The witness is this, that God has given us eternal life, and this life is in His Son. He who has the Son has the life; he who does not have the Son of God does not have the life. These things I have written to you who believe in the name of the Son of God, in order that you may *know* that you have eternal life (1 John 5:11–13).

That's right—the man or woman who personally receives Christ as Savior and Lord is assured of everlasting life with Him in heaven. So, in summary, when you received Christ by faith, as an act of your will, many wonderful things happened including the following:

1. Christ came into your life (Revelation 3:20 and Colossians 1:27).
2. Your sins were forgiven (Colossians 1:14).
3. You became a child of God (John 1:12).
4. You received eternal life (John 5:24).

5. You began the great adventure for which God created you (John 10:10; 1 Thessalonians 5:18).

If you would like free literature to help you grow in your new walk with God, please write to me:

Vonette Bright
Campus Crusade for Christ International
100 Lake Hart Drive, Dept. 2100
Orlando, FL 32832-0100

I would be delighted to send you home study material that will help you understand your new relationship with God; understand His Word, the Bible; and enable you to start in your new life with Him.

Notes

Ney Bailey

1. Portions of this chapter were adapted from *Faith Is Not a Feeling* by Ney Bailey (San Bernardino, CA: Here's Life Publishers, 1978). Used by permission.

Jill Briscoe

1. Portions of this chapter were adapted from *Thank You For Being a Friend* by Jill Briscoe (Grand Rapids, MI: Zondervan, 1980), pp. 180–192. Used by permission.

Sally Christon Conway

1. Portions of this chapter were adapted from *Your Husband's Mid-Life Crisis* by Sally Conway (Elgin, IL: David C. Cook Publishing Co., 1987), pp. 13,14 and *What God Gives When Life Takes* by Becki Conway Sanders and Jim and Sally Conway (Downers Grove, IL: InterVarsity Press, 1988), p. 36. Both used by permission.

Ruth Bell Graham

1. Titus 2:3–5.
2. Portions of this chapter were adapted from *It's My Turn* by Ruth Bell Graham (Old Tappan, NJ: Fleming H. Revell, 1982), pp. 131,136,137. Used by permission.

Joyce Rogers

1. Andrew Murray, *The Believer's Secret of Waiting on God* (Minneapolis: Bethany House Publishers, 1986), pp. 68,69.
2. Murray, *The Believer's Secret*, pp. 67,68.
3. Murray, *The Believer's Secret*, p. 57.

Edith Schaeffer

1. Portions of this chapter are adapted from *L'Abri* by Edith Schaeffer (Wheaton, IL: Tyndale House Publishers, 1969). Used by permission.

Bringing It All Together

1. The four principles are adapted from *Would You Like to Know God Personally?* (*NewLife* Publications, 1995). Used by permission.

Resources

Resources by Vonette Bright

The Joy of Hospitality: Fun Ideas for Evangelistic Entertaining. Co-written with Barbara Ball, this practical book tells how to share your faith through hosting barbecues, coffees, holiday parties, and other events in your home.

The Joy of Hospitality Cookbook. Filled with uplifting Scriptures and quotations, this cookbook contains hundreds of delicious recipes, hospitality tips, sample menus, and family traditions that are sure to make your entertaining a memorable and eternal success. Co-written with Barbara Ball.

Beginning Your Journey of Joy. This adaptation of the *Four Spiritual Laws* speaks in the language of today's women and offers a slightly feminine approach to sharing God's love with your neighbors, friends, and family members.

Resources for Evangelism

Witnessing Without Fear. This best-selling, Gold Medallion book offers simple hands-on, step-by-step coaching on how to share your faith with confidence. The chapters give specific answers to questions people most often encounter in witnessing and provide a proven method for sharing your faith.

Reaching Your World Through Witnessing Without Fear. This six-session video provides the resources needed to sensitively share the gospel effectively. Each session begins with a captivating dramatic vignette to help viewers apply the training. Available in individual study and group packages.

Have You Heard of the Four Spiritual Laws? This booklet is one of the most effective evangelistic tools ever developed. It presents a clear explanation of the gospel of Jesus Christ, which helps you open a conversation easily and share your faith with confidence.

Would You Like to Know God Personally? Based on the *Four Spiritual Laws*, this booklet uses a friendly, conversational format to present four principles for establishing a personal relationship with God.

Jesus and the Intellectual. Drawing from the works of notable scholars who affirm their faith in Jesus Christ, this booklet shows that Christianity is based on irrefutable historical facts. Good for sharing with unbelievers and new Christians.

A Great Adventure. Written as from one friend to another, this booklet explains how to know God personally and experience peace, joy, meaning, and fulfillment in life.

Sharing Christ Using the Four Spiritual Laws (audio cassette). Imagine being personally trained by Bill Bright to use the remarkable *Four Spiritual Laws* booklet. Through a five-part teaching series on WorldChangers Radio, this cassette will increase your confidence level and desire to share the good news with those you know.

Would You Like to Belong to God's Family? Designed for elementary-age young people, this booklet gives the simple message of salvation and includes the first steps for starting their new life in Christ. (Based on the *Four Spiritual Laws*.)

GOD: Discover His Character. Everything about our lives is influenced by our view of God. Through these pages Dr. Bright will equip you with the biblical truths that will energize your walk with God. So when you're confused, you can experience His truth. When you're frightened, you can know His peace. When you're sad, you can live in His joy.

GOD: Discover His Character Video Series. In these 13 sessions, Dr. Bright's clear teaching is illustrated by fascinating dramas that bring home the truth of God's attributes in everyday life. This video series, with the accompanying leader's guide, is ideal for youth, college, and adult Sunday school classes or study groups.

> **Our Great Creator (Vol. I).** Dr. Bright explores God as all-powerful, ever-present, all-knowing, and sovereign, and how those attributes can give you hope and courage.

> **Our Perfect Judge (Vol. II).** God your perfect Judge, is holy, true, righteous, and just, and Dr. Bright explains how those characteristics help you to live a righteous life.

> **Our Gracious Savior (Vol. III).** Dr. Bright introduces you to the God who is loving, merciful, faithful, and unchangeable, and shows how you can experience those awesome attributes every day.

GOD: Discover His Character Audio Edition. Based on the *GOD: Discover His Character* video series, Dr. Bright's insights into God's wondrous character are certain to attract many non-Christians to faith, and to energize the walk of many believers. In each of 15 dynamic messages, Bill Freeman, familiar voice of Campus Crusade's WorldChangers Radio, enhances the learning experience with practical life application questions.

GOD: Knowing Him by His Names. *El-Elyon, Adonai, Jehovah-Sabaoth.* To most Christians, the Hebrew names of God are unknown and unpronounceable. In this compact overview of the meaning and significance of God's names, you will not only learn more about our heavenly Father, but also become more worshipful of His nature. The booklet includes 16 character-revealing names of God, as well as the names of Christ.

GOD: Seeking Him Wholeheartedly. Based on the Great Commandment, recorded in Matthew 22:36,37 ("Love the Lord your God with all your heart..."), this booklet explains seven steps for seeking God with a whole heart. Bill Bright deals with the sincerity of our love for God, the priority of our relationship with Him, and the evidence of our wholehearted devotion—obedience. His insights enable any follower of Christ to grow closer to our heavenly Father and enjoy the fullness of His blessings.

GOD: 13 Steps to Discovering His Attributes. In this abbreviated guide to discovering God's attributes, Dr. Bill Bright shares the fruit of his lifelong study of God. These wonderful truths are certain to enrich your life and energize your walk with God. Keep this handy booklet in your pocket or purse to read during quiet moments, or to share with friends or loved ones.

GOD: Discover the Benefits of His Attributes. As an individual resource, or as a companion to *GOD: Discover His Character* or *GOD: 13 Steps to Discovering His Attributes*, this sturdy, four-color laminated card will energize your Christian life as you're frequently reminded of God's amazing character. Just 3" × 5", it makes a great bookmark, slips easily into purse or pocket, and is conveniently sized to share with friends.

Response Form

☐ I have received Jesus Christ as my Savior and Lord as a result of reading this book.

☐ With God's help, I will faithfully pray for revival, the harvest, laborers, and donors.

☐ I want to be one of the two million people who will join Dr. Bright in forty days of prayer and fasting for revival for America, the world, and the fulfillment of the Great Commission.

☐ Please send me *free* information on ☐ full-time staff, ☐ mid-career change, ☐ associate, ☐ volunteer, ☐ short-term trips, or ☐ summer intern opportunities with Campus Crusade for Christ International.

☐ Please send me *free* information about the other books, booklets, audio cassettes, and videos by Bill and Vonette Bright.

NAME (please print)

ADDRESS

CITY   STATE   ZIP

COUNTRY   E-MAIL

Please check the appropriate box(es), clip, and mail this form to:

> Vonette Bright
> Campus Crusade for Christ
> P.O. Box 620877
> Orlando, FL 32862-0877 U.S.A.

You may also fax your response to (407) 826-2149, or send E-mail to newlifepubs@ccci.org. Visit our websites at www.newlifepubs.com, www.discovergod.org, and www.rsm.org.

This and other fine products from *NewLife* Publications are available from your favorite bookseller or by calling **(800) 235-7255** (within U.S.) or **(407) 826-2145** (outside U.S.).